Guide to ALGOL 6

For Users of RS Systems

Philip M Woodward and
Susan G Bond

Edward Arnold

© South West Universities Regional Computer Centre 1983

First published 1983
by Edward Arnold (Publishers) Ltd
41 Bedford Square London WC1B 3DQ

British Library Cataloguing in Publication Data
Woodward, Philip M.
    Guide to ALGOL 68 for users of RS systems.
    1. ALGOL (Computer program language)
    I. Title   II. Bond, Susan G.
    001.64'24   QA76.73.A24
    ISBN 0 7131 3490 9

Text set in 10/12 pt Linotron 202 Times, printed and bound
in Great Britain at The Pitman Press, Bath

Preface

This Guide is addressed to users of 'RS' Algol 68 systems*. The language adheres closely to the official definition† and the small divergences peculiar to RS systems are noted as such in the text. No significant variations should be found between one RS system and another apart from those directly related to hardware features such as character sets or wordlengths. Uniformity has been a basic design aim for RS systems, and it stems from the use of a single compiler common to all. This compiler, produced by the Royal Signals and Radar Establishment, bears no relation to the older Algol 68-R compiler (also from RSRE).

Each RS system includes a considerable body of software in addition to the compiler, much of it machine-dependent, such as the 'translator' which generates code for a particular type of computer. To avoid unintentional diversity from this source, RS translator writers belong to a coordinating body, the RS Implementors' Group (RIG) under the auspices of the South West Universities Regional Computer Centre.

In writing the Guide, we have assumed that the reader's prime concern is to use Algol 68 for practical programming. No knowledge of other languages is assumed, but some general knowledge of computing is taken for granted. The Guide can be read as a narrative, but is also intended to serve as a programmers' companion afterwards. The indexing and grouping of topics has been influenced by this intended use. Technicalities of language description have been kept within reasonable bounds and details of little practical utility are not exhaustively pursued. However, the structural principles of Algol 68 *must* be carefully studied if the rich rewards the language offers are to be reaped.

It is a pleasure for the authors to acknowledge the numerous facts, comments and suggestions received from Messrs G J Finnie, J Rees, A A Pryor and C Massey of SWURCC, J R Douglas and R L Hutchings of Oxford University, and R J Granville and N E Peeling of RSRE. Finally, we wish to record appreciation to Mrs D Laidlay of SWURCC for word-processing, to Mr Martyn Thomas, Deputy Director of SWURCC, for his constant practical help and encouragement, and to International Computers Limited for financial support of the authors' work.

P M W, S G B
Malvern, January 1982

* The first RS systems were those for the ICL 2900 Series, and the Honeywell Multics.

† *Revised Report on the Algorithmic Language ALGOL 68*, by A van Wijngaarden, B J Mailloux, J E L Peck, C H A Koster, M Sintzoff, C H Lindsey, L J L T Meertens and R G Fisker; *Acta Informatica*, vol 5 parts 1, 2, 3 (1975); Springer-Verlag (Berlin, Heidelberg, New York, 1976); Sigplan Notices of ACM, vol 12 no 5 (May 1977).

Contents

Introduction

Algol 68 is a language which is outstanding in its ability to express the *structural* aspects of a program and its data. This is always important, and in large projects crucial. However, the rewards Algol 68 offers are not gained without some initial effort, even by programmers already well experienced in the use of high level languages. For those coming new to Algol 68, the groundwork covered in Chapters 1 to 3 must be regarded as essential reading. The subsequent chapters should be found relatively straightforward once the design philosophy of the language has been grasped.

For structural purposes, the most important grammatical device is 'nesting'. Modules of program which have been separately compiled can be nested one within another. Within a module, a program is written as a sequence of steps within which other sequences may be nested. The key grammatical unit throughout is the *enclosed clause*, of which loops and conditionals are examples. Such clauses can include one or more sequences of steps, some of which may themselves be enclosed clauses, and so on. A complicated program thus takes on a hierarchical structure with its main features at outer levels and the finer details at inner levels. The same general principle applies to data. A structured object of data has component parts which may themselves be structured to whatever depth may be required.

A flavour of Algol 68 may be gained from the following complete though trivial program, which inputs 500 numbers and outputs their total.

```
PROGRAM sum
BEGIN
    REAL total;
    total := 0;
    REAL x;
    TO 500 DO
            read(x);
            total + := x
        OD;
    write(total)
END
FINISH
```

Indenting shows the different levels of nesting, here only two. Leaving aside the first and last lines (which control the RS compiling system), the program is an enclosed clause bracketed by the special words BEGIN and END. Within this clause there are five steps,

> let 'total' be a real variable;
> set total to zero;
> let 'x' be another real variable;
> loop;
> print accumulated total

The loop is another enclosed clause containing two steps bracketed by the special words DO and OD. The preamble 'TO 500' means that the two steps

> read a number into x;
> increase total by x

are to be repeated 500 times.

One or two details in this example are worth covering straight away—though all factual points are covered again in the main chapters of the Guide. The use of upper and lower case alphabets is not just ornamental. Algol 68 uses two alphabets so that fixed structural words like BEGIN and END are kept distinct from words like 'total' or 'x'. The latter are *identifiers*, whose purpose is to name variables and other objects in the program. The semi-colon is an important punctuation mark used exclusively to prevent two adjacent steps at the same hierarchical level from running together. (That is why there is no semi-colon after the last step inside an enclosed clause.) Layout of the program is ignored by the compiler, and steps do not have to be on separate lines. However, layout is of the highest importance for intelligibility, and should always be designed to show at a glance where any enclosed clauses begin and end.

Accounts of Algol 68 abound in the use of technical terms and words which look like English but which have acquired technical meanings. This can prove a source of irritation to the practical programmer, who has little wish to learn a special language description language as well as Algol 68. In this Guide, therefore, the use of special technical terms is kept to a minimum, but many have become standard and their use unavoidable. These words and phrases are listed in the Glossary, with brief definitions. Again for simplicity, we have avoided formal tables of syntax, as the Glossary can fulfil the same function. A quick syntactic outline of the language can be obtained by looking up the entry for 'enclosed clause' and pursuing all the various possibilities.

1 The classification of objects

1.1 Mode checking

A computer program starts with objects of data and describes the operations to be carried out on them. The objects need not be arithmetical values. They could be reference numbers, book titles, or data structures with many component parts, some numerical, some non-numerical. Operations appropriate for one kind of object, such as addition and subtraction, might not be appropriate for another—or might need special redefinition. With all the possible variety of objects, some degree of control over their handling is essential. One of the main functions of a high level language is to impose such control, and the method used in Algol 68 is based on a comprehensive classification scheme. Every object has a 'mode' to describe its nature. Modes for commonly occurring objects are laid down as part of the language. The mode of a whole number or integer is INT (and the abbreviation is compulsory). That of a more general type of number which might have a fractional part is REAL. The mode of a character such as a letter of the alphabet is CHAR, and that of a logical or boolean value, meaning TRUE or FALSE, is BOOL. More complicated types of object require more complicated modes, and the programmer is free to build these up from the given starting modes using methods to be outlined by examples in the present chapter.

The part played by modes in Algol 68 must be understood in relation to the contexts in which objects are used. There are many different types of context in a computer program. To take just one example, the objects x and y in a formula such as x + y are in 'operand' positions, being operands of the plus operator. The modes of operands are checked by the compiler to ensure that they suit the given operator, and that the correct meaning of the operator is taken. Whatever the position of an object, its mode is compared with the modes which the context would find acceptable. A disparity does not necessarily imply error, as an object can be converted into an object of a related mode which would be suitable. This is called *coercion*. As an example, the INT value 3 would be coerced to the REAL value 3.0 in a context which insisted on a REAL—a coercion called 'widening', because real numbers are a wider class than integers. Some contexts are more demanding than others. A 'strong' context accepts one mode of object only, and causes all types of coercion to be applied. Other contexts make weaker demands, as the mode of the object may contribute to the meaning of the program in some significant way. Less coercion is then possible. When a program is compiled, the modes of all the objects are thoroughly checked in relation to context. If disparities are found which are beyond the powers of coercion to remedy, they are reported as faults. For an example, we need look no further than a REAL in a strong INT context. This gives rise to a fault because there is no type of coercion which will convert a REAL to an INT. It is not considered reasonable to round off fractional parts on the quiet. To convert a real number to an integer, one or other of the available operators (ROUND or ENTIER) must be used explicitly.

In practice, the classification of objects by their modes imposes a discipline on the programmer which is easily acquired and encourages clear thinking. When programming mistakes are made, as they always will be, the system of mode checking helps to make them detectable at an early stage. Because it knows about the nature of every object, the compiler can detect all obvious inconsistencies in the handling of objects before a program is allowed to run.

In this Guide, modes are printed in upper case type. Formal Algol 68 requires two distinct alphabets, one used mainly for the identification of objects (x, y, pi) and the other for modes and special words such as IF and BEGIN. It is customary to use bold face type as the second alphabet in published programs. Here, however, the ordinary upper case alphabet is used instead of bold words to conform with character sets of actual computers. Where a computer system does not offer the use of two alphabets, makeshift arrangements can always be made (Appendix 1).

1.2 Single objects, arrays and structures

Objects can be used singly or in groups which are themselves classed as objects. A single object with a simple mode can, if its value is known when the program is written, be represented in the program as a *denotation*. Examples are shown below.

mode	INT	REAL	CHAR	BOOL
denotation	6	0.5	","	TRUE

The forms of denotations are given in detail in Appendix 2, and are so designed that the modes are unambiguous. However, it is worth pointing out that objects may be represented slightly differently in data streams read by programs.

Single objects can be combined to form larger composite objects in two distinct ways. The more familiar type of grouping is the *array*. This is a set of objects all of the same mode, such as the twelve integers

31	28	31	30	31	30	31	31	30	31	30	31

As a one-dimensional array of integers, this set has mode [ ]INT, pronounced 'row of int'. A row can be of any length down to one element or even none at all, and the actual size need not be known when the program is written. It can be a computed quantity. An element of a row is picked out when required by means of a 'subscript' which gives the position of the element in the sequence. The position can be chosen dynamically, that is by computing the value of the subscript in the program. Arrays can have any number of dimensions; for example the mode of a two-dimensional array of real numbers is [,]REAL, pronounced 'row row of real', and the mode of a three-dimensional array of reals is [, ,]REAL, pronounced 'row row row of real'. The elements of an array can be of any mode whatsoever. A row of rows of characters, for instance, would have mode [ ][ ]CHAR, pronounced 'row of row of kar'.

The other type of grouping is the *structure*, differing from the array in two respects. The component parts, called fields, can have assorted modes but cannot be selected dynamically. Turning to music for an example, in the first complete gramophone recording of Wagner's Siegfried, Act 1 occupies 3 long playing record sides and lasts for a total of 82.3 minutes. The two parts of this data can be kept together by using a mode such as

STRUCT(INT sides, REAL minutes)

The structure contains one integer field and one real field, identified by the field selectors 'sides' and 'minutes'. Though not in upper case type, these selectors are in fact an integral part of the mode. Consequently a context which expected to find an object of the above mode but found, let us say, one of mode

STRUCT(INT sides, REAL seconds)

would give rise to a fault. The two modes, having different field selectors, are quite unrelated.

A new name can be introduced for any constructed mode in a step called a 'mode declaration'. Its greatest value is for shortening lengthy structure modes so that they do not have to be written out in full more than once. An example of a mode declaration is

MODE ACT = STRUCT(INT sides, REAL minutes)

Using this mode for one act of an opera (*any* act), the mode for an entire opera could be

[ ]ACT

Such brevity is of the greatest practical value when a data structure is being handled as a whole, as it makes the program more readable.

1.3 Variables and references

In Algol 68, as in other languages, values such as intermediate results can be assigned to variables for safe keeping. In formulae, variables serve as names for these values. However, Algol 68 makes a significant distinction between the variable and the value it holds for reasons we shall shortly see. The variable is said to *refer* to the value, and its mode starts with the word REF. Thus a variable holding an INT has mode REF INT, and similarly for all other modes. New variables are introduced into a program by steps called *variable declarations*, of which

REAL x

is an example. This step does two related things; it sets aside space for the holding of a REAL and it defines x as the variable of mode REF REAL. Remember always that modes are thoroughly checked when an Algol 68 program is compiled. This prevents the assignment of any value other than a REAL to the variable x. An assignment is a step such as

    x : = 1.0

which makes x refer to 1.0 in place of any value which may have been assigned previously. Before any assignment has been made to a new variable, the value to which it refers is indeterminate. To avoid any risk of using such a value in error, a variable declaration can include an initial assignment, such as

    REAL x : = 0.0

all in one step. This step does three things; it sets aside space for a REAL, defines x as a real variable (a REF REAL), and assigns 0.0 to it.

The pattern is much the same for variables of all kinds. In all cases, the mode written in the variable declaration is that of the value to be held. One extra thing may be necessary. When an array variable is being declared, the size of the array must be given so that the required amount of space can be set aside. The size is placed in the square brackets of the array mode, but it is not part of the mode as such. As an example, the declaration

    [7]REAL w

sets aside space for the 7-element array of mode [ ]REAL; the mode of the array variable w is REF[ ]REAL.

The concept of a reference as an object in its own right is important. As just one illustration, imagine a problem which calls for a number of bulky items of data to be held in different sequences in a number of separate arrays. Each array is to hold exactly the same items, but the ordering is to be different. Copies of each item could be held in the various arrays, but this is wasteful of space. It is more compact and more convenient to hold one copy of each item and then work with references to it. Typically, the mode of an array of references to structured items would be

    [ ]REF STRUCT(... ... ...)

However large a structure may be, a reference to it takes up only a small fixed amount of space.

The power to manipulate references raises the question of what, in any given context, a variable actually stands for. The general rule in Algol 68 is to treat references as references whenever the context will accept them. For example, the left-hand side of the assignment

    x : = 1.0

assumes that x is a reference and uses it as such. But the formula

    x + 1.0

cannot use x as a reference. References are not numerical objects and cannot be operated on arithmetically. In this context, therefore, x is replaced by the value to which it refers. Such replacement is called *dereferencing*, and is the commonest form of coercion.

To work with references freely, it is just as necessary to have variables for holding them as to have ordinary variables for holding numbers. Thus

REF REAL r

declares r as a variable which can hold a REF REAL. The mode of r is REF REF REAL. As another example,

REF[ ]REAL s

declares s as a REF REF[ ]REAL, capable of holding any reference to a row of reals. An assignment such as

s := w

where w is the variable declared earlier in this section would therefore be perfectly legal. Notice that it is not possible to declare a variable which can hold *any* reference. The mode must be fully specified; references such as REF INT, REF REAL, REF[ ]REAL, are all quite distinct.

Modes starting with a single REF are of course commonplace. Double references are by no means unusual, and every Algol 68 programmer should become familiar with their use (Chapter 6). A whole class of applications exploits triple references (also described in Chapter 6), but quadruple references never seem to be required in practice.

1.4 Procedures

A procedure is an object which can be *obeyed*. It is a piece of program packaged so that it can be obeyed in any number of different places using only one copy of the text. It nearly always has its own identifier, like 'sqrt' which identifies the piece of program for finding square roots. The mode of a procedure always begins PROC, and the continuation specifies how it is meant to interface with its context when it is obeyed or 'called'. If it needs to be given any objects to work on (i.e. parameters), their modes must be listed in parentheses with commas for separation. The mode concludes with the mode of the result yielded by the procedure when it is obeyed. Thus the mode of sqrt is

PROC(REAL)REAL

because sqrt must be given a REAL parameter (a number to take the square root of) and will deliver a REAL result. The assignments in the following variable declarations illustrate calls of sqrt.

REAL x := sqrt(81);
REAL y := sqrt(x)

Both of these procedure calls give rise to coercions. The parameter in a procedure call is in a strong context because its mode has already been laid down as part of the mode of the procedure. The parameter of sqrt must be a REAL, and yet 81 is an INT and x is a REF REAL. In a strong context, an INT can be widened to a REAL, and this makes sqrt(81) acceptable. Similarly, a REF REAL will be dereferenced to give back 9.0 which is then given over to sqrt. This delivers the real result 3.0 for assignment to y.

It can be seen that a procedure call involves mode checking, and the remarks made in Section 1.1 are particularly relevant. If the parameter supplied to a procedure has entirely the wrong mode, a fault is reported. Coercion only takes place for closely related modes where the conversion would be reasonable.

A procedure can do useful work without delivering any result at all to the context. For example, a procedure 'inflate' could be written to increase the value held in some real variable by some given percentage, but deliver no explicit result. With the variable and the percentage as parameters (in that order), the mode of 'inflate' would be defined as

PROC(REF REAL, REAL)VOID

The first parameter has the mode of a variable, REF REAL, because the procedure assigns a new value to it. The effect of the following steps would be to write out 1.44.

REAL x : = 1.0;
inflate (x, 20);
inflate (x, 20);
write (x)

The parameters in a procedure call must, of course, be given in the right order. The use of inflate (20, x) would cause the compiler to report a mode error, as the integer 20 cannot be coerced to mode REF REAL. (Nor could the real number 20.0.) References cannot be created by coercions.

The modes of the procedures 'write' for output, and its converse 'read' for input, are not revealed in this Guide, but they both start with PROC and end with VOID, showing that no results are delivered to their contexts.

Procedures are, naturally enough, meant to be obeyed. But they can also be handled as objects in various ways. Procedure variables can be declared, and have procedures assigned to them—provided that the modes agree properly. A procedure can be a field of a structure, a facility found to be of great utility in systems programming. But perhaps most important of all, a procedure can be supplied as a parameter of another procedure, which can then obey it in contexts and with parameters of its own choosing. Procedures for finding the area under unspecified mathematical curves are usually designed in this way. For example, a procedure p having the mode

PROC(PROC(REAL)REAL, REAL, REAL)REAL

could find the area under a mathematical function represented by a PROC(REAL) REAL between two given REAL limits. The call

p(sqrt, 1.0, 2.0)

would then give as its result the area under the graph of sqrt(x) between 1.0 and 2.0.

2 The steps in a program

2.1 Introduction

An Algol 68 program to be compiled in one piece by an RS system is written in the form

> PROGRAM *identifier*
> *enclosed clause*
> FINISH

where the *identifier* serves as the title of the program. The *enclosed clause* is the body of the Algol 68 program proper, and normally consists of a *series* of steps separated by semi-colons and all enclosed in brackets. The brackets can be ordinary round brackets, or more prominently BEGIN and END, which are equivalent.

> BEGIN
>   *step;*
>   . . .
>   *step;*
>   *step*
> END

A *step* is either a *declaration* or a *unit* (sometimes called a unitary clause). A declaration is a step in which the programmer can define a new identifier, mode name or operator. A unit describes some actual computing to be carried out. Declarations and units can be interspersed in a series, but in RS systems anything the programmer wishes to declare must be declared before it is first used.

Consecutive steps in a series must be separated by semi-colons. This important syntax rule emphasizes the fact that the successive steps are quite distinct. If a step computes some value which will be needed in a later step—even if it is the very next step—the value must be put away safely first. If this is not done in the original step, e.g. by assigning the value to a variable, the value will be lost. The semi-colon in Algol 68 discards any result which may be in hand at the completion of a step in order to make way for the step which follows. The *final* step in a series must be a unit and must not be followed by a semi-colon, about which more later. A semi-colon before the word END is an error of syntax, for END is not a step.

The class of constructions which fall under the heading of 'units' is very wide, and the contexts in which they will fit are numerous. An assignment is a common type of unit, being particularly useful as a step in a series for the reasons already explained. Another and simpler type of unit is an expression, such as sqrt(x) or n + 2, where the intention is simply to obtain a result. Units of this kind might be pointless as program steps but are essential in the many other contexts in which units are allowed to appear. For example, a parameter in a procedure call can be a unit, and the right-hand side of an assignment can be a unit.

The fact that the results of intermediate steps in a series are discarded does not altogether invalidate the use of expressions as steps in a program. Unlike sqrt(x) or n + 2, some expressions take an action of some kind rather than produce a result. (Many expressions do both.) As a simple example, we may consider the procedure call 'write(x)'. This has the same syntactic form as sqrt(x). Both are simple cases of expressions, but unlike sqrt(x), write(x) has as its purpose an action quite different from computing a value. It does not deliver any result to its context in the program, and when followed by a semi-colon, nothing at all is lost.

As already stated, a complete program is normally written as a bracketed series of steps, but this same type of construction can also be used in many contexts *within* a program—including places where values are expected. The value of a series used in this way is taken as the value of its final step, and this topic forms the subject matter for Chapter 3. The present chapter deals only with the elementary steps which form the basic building bricks for larger constructions. Declarations for identifiers are described in Section 2.2, and the two commonest types of unit—expressions and assignments—in Sections 2.3 and 2.4.

2.2 Declaration of identifiers

Identifiers stand for objects. They are mnemonic sequences of lower case letters and digits, starting with a letter. In RS systems they must be declared before they are used. Some identifiers (such as read, write, sqrt, pi) are already declared before the start of the user's own program—in what is called the standard prelude—but the same principle applies. No unknown identifiers can be used. Excluded from present consideration are labels (Section 3.5) and field selectors (Section 6.2), which have the same form as identifiers but are entirely different entities. They do not stand for objects, and are therefore not identifiers in the proper sense of the word.

After declaration, an identifier is known and can be used throughout a certain range of the program. This range is defined in Chapter 3 for all situations; it always includes the remaining steps of the current series, and may extend further. The same identifier cannot be declared twice for the same range.

Identifiers can be declared in two ways. For variables, the most convenient type of declaration is the *variable declaration* (2.2.1). For other objects such as constants, *identity declarations* are used (2.2.2). The identity declaration is in fact a more fundamental feature of Algol 68 than the variable declaration. It can be used to declare identifiers for objects of all modes, including variables, a point further pursued in the next chapter (3.2.2).

2.2.1 Variable declarations
A variable declaration creates space in which any object of the mode stated can be held, and defines the identifier as the reference to that object. Thus

REAL x : = 0.0

creates space for a REAL, declares x as the REF REAL and assigns 0.0 as the initial value of the REAL. Initialization is optional, so there are two forms of variable declaration:

mode identifier := *unit*

or *mode identifier*

When the mode is that of an array, information about the size of the array must be inserted in the square brackets so that the right amount of space can be created.

In the initialized declaration, the *unit* is usually some simple expression. It is evaluated to yield an object of the mode written on the left-hand side, and then assigned. Because the mode is known, the unit is in a strong context where all forms of coercion can be applied. In a variable declaration, it must always be remembered that the mode of the variable itself is REF to the mode actually written on the left-hand side.

Several variables, individually initialized or not initialized, can be declared in one step provided that the same mode applies to all. The mode is written once, and the individual items following it are separated by commas, as shown below:

```
INT n, m := 0;
read(n);
[n]REAL x, y;
    . . .
```

In the first line, zero is assigned to m, but n is not initialized. In the third line, the array variables (mode REF[ ]REAL) each make space for the holding of n reals.

When several declarations are combined in one step, they are dealt with in an undefined order, so the identifiers cannot be regarded as declared until the end of the step as a whole. Thus, in a situation such as

REAL x := *unit*, y := *unit*

the second unit must not attempt to use the variable x.

2.2.2 Identity declarations

An identity declaration is used when an identifier is needed for an object which already exists or can be suitably expressed. It may be a simple constant of mode REAL, an array, a structure, an existing reference, a procedure—in fact anything. As an example, the following identity declaration

REAL inch = 25.4

makes 'inch' synonymous with the constant 25.4. The mode of 'inch' is REAL. No new object has been created; just another way of writing 25.4. Having mode REAL, 'inch' cannot be used as a variable, and no value (not even 25.4) can be assigned to it. Any attempt to do so would cause a fault. For an example applied to references, suppose that x is an existing real variable. Then

REF REAL y = x

defines the identifier y as the very same REF REAL. The two identifiers are not distinct variables, but just alternative names attached to the same working space. This type of declaration can be useful when the right-hand side is a more elaborate kind of unit such as a subscripted array variable (as in Section 4.3.1) or a procedure call delivering a reference as its result.

Other examples of identity declarations are

    INT n = 2358072
    CHAR point = "."
    BOOL vrai = TRUE

In all these examples, the right-hand sides are denotations, i.e. representations of actual objects. More general expressions are, of course, permitted. Grammatically, the form of an identity declaration is

    mode identifier   =   unit

The *mode* must never include any array size information, as the left-hand side does not create a new object or generate new space. The *unit* must deliver a result of the specified mode, and is thus in a strong context. All forms of coercion will, if necessary, be applied. When a result of the required mode has been reached, the identifier is made synonymous with it.

Several identity declarations can be combined in one step provided that the mode is the same in each, but identity declarations and variable declarations cannot be mixed. As an example,

    [ ]CHAR c = "carbon", h = "hydrogen"

declares the identifiers c and h to have modes [ ]CHAR and to stand for 'carbon' and 'hydrogen'. In any composite declaration, the identifiers must not be regarded as declared until the end of the step as a whole.

Although data for a problem should normally be read in by the program, there are often many constants (or numbers which are thought to be unlikely to change) which can reasonably be written into the program as denotations. The use of identity declarations to provide such constants with identifiers is always worth considering. The identifiers serve as a reminder of their meanings, and also guarantee exact repetition of their values. Furthermore, if a change should be required to any 'constant', its appearance in only one place simplifies any subsequent editing of the program text.

The close similarity in appearance between the initialized variable declaration and the identity declaration (: = in one, = in the other) is one of the less fortunate aspects of Algol 68 symbolism. It is useful to remember that the mode actually written in either kind of declaration is the mode of result to be delivered by the right-hand side. In an identity declaration, the identifier has this very mode. In a variable declaration, the mode of the identifier is REF to the mode actually written.

2.3 Expressions

An expression is one sort of *unit*. It is not too misleading to think of it as a construction designed to produce a result, even though some expressions may not do so. (Such expressions can be said to have results of mode VOID.) With this in mind, it seems natural that an expression should consist of a single term, known as a primary, or a formula made up of primaries and operators. An expression can also include generators and items selected from structures. In this chapter, we concentrate on primaries and formulae, deferring the subject of generators to Section 3.2.2 and selections to Chapter 6.

2.3.1 Primaries

As a syntactic term, 'primary' means the starting point for building up larger constructions. A primary is any simple compact item, or any item in brackets. A complete list of primaries is given in the following table.

Primary	Example	Reference
denotation	68	Appendix 2
identifier	algol 68	Section 2.2
procedure call	sqrt(x)	Chapter 5
slice of array	v[4]	Chapter 4
enclosed clause	(a + b + c)	Chapter 3 and below
cast	[ ]INT(3, 5, 7)	see below
format text	$ 20*k* 3*d* $	Chapter 7

Some of these primaries have not yet been described at all. A *slice* is a primary representing an array, followed by a square bracketed construction called an indexer. This combination is used for the purpose of selecting some subset of a given array—or just a single element of it. The indexer gives all the subscripting information required to define the slice. An *enclosed clause* is a bracketed construction such as a term in round brackets in a formula. Enclosed clauses using round and other types of bracket also play an important role in the structuring of a program, as described in Chapter 3. The remaining type of enclosed clause in this Guide is the *collateral display*, which is used to display all the elements of a row or fields of a structure, as in the following identity declarations:

```
[ ]INT days  =  (31, 28, 31, 30, 31, 30, 31, 31, 30, 31, 30, 31)
STRUCT(INT sides,  REAL minutes)act2  =  (3, 74.3)
```

The items in a collateral display are units. A collateral display can only be used in a strong row or structure context where the mode is completely determined. This may entail the use of a 'cast', which is another primary construction.

A *cast* is a way of artificially introducing a strong context, to force some required coercion or coercions to take place. The cast is written as a mode—the mode actually required—followed by the object to be coerced, which must be placed in brackets (unless it is already expressed as some form of enclosed clause). The mode required must be one which can be reached by coercion: arbitrary mode changes can never take place. Casting is often used to reduce the number of REFs on the left-hand side of an assignment, where dereferencing does not occur spontaneously. The following is an illustration of what is meant. After the declarations

```
REAL x  : =  0.0;
REF REAL xx  : =  x
```

the value held in x can be changed in either of two ways—by direct assignment, such as x := 1.0, or by casting xx to the mode of x:

REF REAL(xx) := 1.0

This may seem obtuse, but realistic examples can be found under the heading of triple references in Chapter 6. Casting, as remarked earlier, is also required to make collateral displays usable in positions which would not otherwise be strong, typically in formulae.

2.3.2 Formulae

In a quite literal sense, the formula is the real scene of *operations* in computing, for every other construction is concerned in some way or another with matters of organization.

The simplest formula consists of a 'monadic' operator—an operator taking one operand—followed by a primary. In the following examples, which show some of the standard monadic operators, x represents a REAL object, n an INT and b a BOOL:

−x	result is x with opposite sign
ROUND x	result is the integer closest to x
ODD n	produces as its result the boolean TRUE
	if n is odd, and FALSE otherwise
NOT b	produces the boolean result TRUE if b
	is FALSE, and FALSE if b is TRUE

One operator may, as will be seen later, have different meanings for different modes of operand. Its definition includes the mode of the result produced.

Any monadic operator can be applied to the result of some other monadic operation provided that the mode is acceptable, as for example ODD ROUND x. Notice that the operations are actually carried out in the order right to left (x first rounded, then tested for oddness), but the order in which the formula must be written is usually the natural way of thinking.

'Dyadic' operators are those which take two operands, one on each side of the operator, as for example

x∗y	x times y
x/y	x divided by y
x∗∗n	x raised to the integer power n

Again the operands may be primaries or the results of other operations—monadic or dyadic. When more than one operator is involved, brackets may be used to force the required grouping of terms, as in the formula (x+y)∗(x−y), but in the absence of brackets the following rules are applied.

1   The binding of a monadic operator to its operand is tighter than any dyadic binding. Thus

− x ∗∗ n means (−x) ∗∗ n

The minus operator here is monadic. Plus and minus can be monadic or dyadic.

2   Every dyadic operator has a priority number in the range 1 to 9, and the larger the number, the tighter the binding. Some examples are

operator	OR	AND	=	<	>	+	−	*	/	**
priority	2	3	4	5	5	6	6	7	7	8

It follows that x + y ∗ z means x + (y ∗ z) as it would do in ordinary mathematics. It is instructive to compare the formula

0 − x ∗∗ n

which uses the dyadic minus operator and means 0 − (x ∗∗ n), with the example using monadic minus shown in rule 1.

3   Dyadic operators of equal priority are obeyed in their written order, i.e. left to right. Consequently, x/y ∗ z means (x/y) ∗ z, but in all cases where the meaning seems doubtful, brackets should be used. Superfluous brackets do not introduce any extra overheads into the running program.

Although expressed differently, operators are akin to procedures in the sense that they take one or two operands where a procedure might take one or two parameters. But there is an important difference. At any one time a procedure can have only one definition, and this specifies the modes of the parameters uniquely. The parameters in a procedure call are therefore in strong contexts. This is not the case for operands. An operator can have several definitions in force simultaneously, distinguished by the number of operands (one or two) and their modes. An operand is therefore not in a strong context. Consider, for example, the very simple formula

ABS q

It will be found from Appendix 3 that the operator ABS is defined for operands of mode BOOL, CHAR, INT and REAL, amongst others. The context therefore cannot determine the mode of q, and this limits the types of mode change which can be effected by coercion. In fact, operands are dereferenced as many times as required, but coercions like INT to REAL (widenings) are never carried out. This prohibition enables an operator to use different definitions for INT and REAL operands.

As the definition— or even the existence—of an operator depends on the modes of its operands, care should always be taken. The mode of the result of an operation can be just as important as the modes of operands, as the result of one operation may be the operand of another. Thus the formula a < b < c is meaningless, because a < b yields a boolean result, and the standard operator < is undefined for a boolean operand. The intention of the programmer who writes this construction is probably a < b AND b < c, which is correct without brackets as the priority of < is greater than that of AND.

A complete list of the standard operators and associated priorities is given in Appendix 3. New operators, or new meanings for existing operators, can be declared by the user as described in Section 5.8.

2.4 Assignment

Apart from expressions, the commonest form of unit is an assignment. This causes a given object to be held in a given reference, where it will remain until a fresh assignment is made or the reference itself disappears (Chapter 3). The mode of the reference completely determines the mode of the object which can be held.

An assignment is a unit of the form

> *expression*   : =   *unit*

The *expression* must yield a reference. The expression will usually and most simply be a variable, though it could be a generator or a call of a procedure which delivered a reference. The *unit* on the right-hand side must yield an object whose mode has one less REF than the left-hand side. The right-hand side is therefore a strong context, in which all forms of coercion may be applied. The commonest is dereferencing, as shown in the following episode.

```
REAL x, y;
x := 0.0;
y := x
```

In the third step, x is dereferenced so that a REAL can be assigned to y, whose mode is REF REAL.

In many programming languages, an assignment clause must stand alone as a complete program step. In Algol 68, it can also be a unit embedded in a larger step. In any embedded context, the act of assignment is carried out, and the reference from the left-hand side is then taken to be the result. For example,

```
sqrt (x := 3.0)
```

assigns 3.0 to x and then carries on as though sqrt(x) had been written. This makes the assignment into a kind of side-effect, and is open to criticism on grounds of style, not because nesting is bad but because assignments change the meanings of variables. To do this in the middle of a formula would obviously be dangerous. Less objectionable is the multiple assignment, such as

```
y  :=  x  :=   0.0
```

in place of the two separate assignments in the previous example. This construction is parsed, by the grammar rule for assignment, as

> *expression*   *unit*
>   y   : =   x := 0.0

When the assignment to x has been carried out, the result x is dereferenced, and the REAL value 0.0 assigned to y. It will be seen that multiple assignments are carried out from right to left. An example of multiple assignment in which no coercions are required is seen in

```
REF REAL r;
REAL x;
r := x := 0.0
```

The modes in the double assignment step down one at a time from REF REF REAL through REF REAL to REAL. An assignment such as

   r := 2.0   ???

is wrong because the left-hand side of an assignment is never dereferenced before assignment takes place, and there is no way of converting the REAL on the right to mode REF REAL. It is, of course, possible to force a dereference on the left-hand side by casting:

   REF REAL(r) := 2.0

The modes are now correct, and the effect will be to assign 2.0 to the variable x which had been assigned to r earlier.

2.4.1 Assignment operators
In practice, a very commonly needed type of assignment is

   x := x + h

which increments x by h. Algol 68 provides us with an alternative way of expressing this assignment, one which is usually quicker to write and more efficient to obey, particularly when x is a more complicated primary such as an indexed array or slice. The alternative construction is

   x PLUSAB h

where PLUSAB (alternatively represented by the compound symbol + : =) is intended to suggest 'plus and becomes'. This is not in fact an abbreviated assignment clause but a *formula*, as the upper case word PLUSAB is a dyadic operator. For its left operand it will accept a REF INT or REF REAL (amongst others) and for its right operand a corresponding object suitable for assignment (e.g. not a REAL for assignment to a REF INT). After carrying out the assignment it yields the left operand as the result of the operation. This is similar to the action of an assignment clause, but unlike assignment, PLUSAB will dereference *either or both* of its operands to reach modes for which it is defined.

   Although 'x PLUSAB h' is a formula, it is best treated as if it were a unit, and not mixed up with other primaries and operators in a larger formula. There are two reasons for this. Assignments within formulae are a safety hazard because they can make the order of evaluation critical. And as the priority of PLUSAB is the lowest of all (1), brackets will almost always be needed in a formula. As a unit, however, with primaries as operands, the construction is extremely useful.

   Companion operators to PLUSAB are MINUSAB, TIMESAB and DIVAB. For integer arithmetic, there are also OVERAB and MODAB. Details of all these operators are given in Appendix 3.

3 Enclosed clauses

3.1 Introduction

An *enclosed clause* is a piece of program having a clearly defined beginning and ending. It may be a loop, or a conditional, or simply a bracketed portion of program. It may be short or long, but the fact of its enclosure makes it into a *primary*, which means that it is usable in virtually any context ranging from the entire body of a program down to a single term in a formula. This versatility makes it a powerful structural tool.

The first type of enclosed clause to be considered in this chapter is the *simple closed clause* (as we shall call it, for other accounts of the language use the term 'closed clause'). One application of such a clause has already been met in formulae. For example, in

$$a * b * (x + y)$$

the bracketed factor is a simple closed clause. The purpose here is to impose a desired grouping of terms. The formula could alternatively be written

$$a * b * BEGIN \ x + y \ END$$

but it is more usual to reserve BEGIN and END for bracketing series containing more than just a single step. These larger clauses have a structural significance explained in Section 3.2.

The other types of enclosed clause have extra properties, and some typical forms are shown below.

simple closed clause:	BEGIN	*series*	END			
loop clause:	WHILE	*series*	DO	*series*	OD	
conditional clause:	IF	*series*	THEN	*series*	ELSE *series*	FI

As any step in a series may itself be an enclosed clause, the various different parts of a program can be nested to varying degrees. This is one of the most characteristic features of Algol 68.

3.2 Simple closed clauses

By enclosing a series between BEGIN and END (or round brackets) to form a simple closed clause, a piece of program becomes to some extent self-contained. It can have its own local declarations, but can also use those of the surrounding program. It can deliver a result to its context, the result being defined as that of the final step obeyed. The properties of simple closed clauses are of very general importance, for they apply with minor variations to all types of enclosed clause described in this chapter.

A simple closed clause defines the 'range' of any identifiers, mode names or operator definitions declared within it. At the END of the closed clause, they all lose their meanings. Such localization serves several practical purposes. It limits the numbers of identifiers and definitions simultaneously in use and helps to keep their declarations textually close at hand, both of which are important considerations in large programs. A second important property is that the space created by local variable declarations is released as soon as the variables pass out of range. For large arrays, this can be a significant economy.

If an identifier for local use is the same as one which has already been declared in the surrounding program, the local meaning is taken to apply. The non-local object continues to exist, but becomes temporarily inaccessible. For example, the effect of

```
BEGIN
    INT n := 2;
    BEGIN
        INT n := 1;
        write(n)
    END;
    write(n)
END
```

is to write 1 and then 2.

The result of the last unit obeyed in any series is taken to be the result of the series, and hence of the simple closed clause. For example,

INT i := BEGIN *step* ; *step* ; *step* ; 6 END

assigns 6 to i. A simple closed clause delivering a result is often used as the body of a procedure (Section 5.3), and the result is then the result of the procedure.

3.2.1 Heap variables
The result of a simple closed clause can be an object of any mode, but special consideration must be given to references. Consider the clause

BEGIN REAL x; read(x); x END

In step 1 a local variable has been declared, in step 2 a real number is read into it and in step 3 the local variable is given as the result. If this clause is used in a context which expects a REAL, all is well; x is dereferenced and the REAL delivered. But situations can arise (as we shall find in Chapter 6) where a closed clause is required to deliver as its result a *reference* which has been created within itself. The simple closed clause shown above cannot do this, for although x has mode REF REAL, its space has a lifetime which terminates at the END of the clause, after which the reference is of course meaningless. Indeed, any attempt to use an invalid reference can lead a program badly astray.

At a certain cost in general overheads which vary a little from one Algol 68 implementation to another, space created by a variable declaration can be given a lifetime which extends beyond the range of its identifier. This is done by putting the word HEAP in front of the variable declaration, as in the following simple closed clause.

```
BEGIN
    HEAP INT n;
    . . .
    . . .
    n
END
```

The word HEAP is not part of a mode: it only alters the way in which space is allocated. The range of the identifier n is not altered; it cannot be used after the END of the clause. But the space is not reclaimed at this point, and the REF INT delivered as the result of this clause remains a valid object. It could for example be held in a reference variable previously declared for that purpose, as in the following extract.

```
REF INT refholder;
    . . .
    refholder : =  (HEAP INT n; . . . . . . ; n);
    . . .
```

The 'heap' is an area of store in which space is protected for as long as the program can access it. Not until all references are lost, by fresh assignments to any variables like 'refholder', is space made available for re-use. The mechanism which brings this about is called 'garbage collection'. In view of the possible overheads entailed, the HEAP facility should be used with reasonable discretion.

3.2.2 Generators

Up to this point, the only construction used for creating working space has been the variable declaration. In work which involves manipulation of references as objects, this is not always convenient or possible. Each new reference would need a new identifier, and the number of identifiers has to be fixed when the program is being written. Algol 68 therefore provides a construction called a *generator* which creates space for a given mode of object and supplies the reference without giving it an identifier. By using generators, any number of new references can be created dynamically; in a loop, for example, a generator creates space afresh every time it is obeyed.

A *local generator* is an expression of the form

LOC *mode*

This creates space for an object of the given mode and gives the reference as its result. A generator such as 'LOC REAL' can therefore be used in a context expecting a REF REAL, such as

REF REAL r : = LOC REAL : = 0.0

which is similar to an example in Section 2.4, where an existing variable is used instead of a generator. It is interesting to see that the identity declaration

REF REAL x = LOC REAL

is exactly equivalent to the variable declaration 'REAL x'. Any variable declaration can be regarded as an abbreviated form of identity declaration such as this. The array variable declaration

[100]REAL h

is an abbreviation for

REF[ ]REAL h = LOC[100]REAL

Generators of array space must give the array size as shown here.

The space generated by a local generator is released when the most recently declared identifier (or other symbol) which is currently valid passes out of range. To create space and its associated reference with a lifetime beyond this, a *heap generator* must be used. This is written as HEAP *mode*. The same considerations apply to heap generators as to heap variables (3.2.1). The heap variable declaration

HEAP[6]INT a

is simply an abbreviation for the identity declaration

REF[ ]INT a = HEAP[6]INT

As remarked in the previous section, there are likely to be certain overheads associated with use of the heap system, but these should not be great enough to deter its use when required. Nevertheless, care should always be taken not to hold on to references created by heap generation when they are no longer required, as this prevents the space being reused.

3.3 Looping

A series is obeyed repeatedly without limit if enclosed in the matching brackets DO and OD. To set a limit on the number of repetitions, there are several choices. One of the units between DO and OD could be a jump out (Section 3.5), but other methods are usually preferable. A preamble before DO can give the actual number of repetitions required, or a condition to be satisfied each time round if repetition is to continue. The last of these methods is the most general, and takes the form

WHILE *series* DO *series* OD

The series after WHILE must deliver a result of mode BOOL, which is the condition for continuation. If it is FALSE, the whole clause is abandoned, and the DO part is not obeyed at all. If it is TRUE, the series after DO is obeyed, and the series after WHILE is then obeyed again. The cycle continues until the WHILE part delivers FALSE. The whole clause is then abandoned and the boolean result in hand is discarded. A loop clause never delivers a result to its context.

Either of the series in the above form of loop can, of course, contain declarations. The range of anything declared in the WHILE part is the whole clause (i.e. both of the series), and the range of anything declared in the DO part is that part alone.

   As an example, the following loop reads in a stream of characters up to the first full stop, copying them out as it goes. The full stop is read but not copied. The operator /=, meaning not equals, can take operands of mode CHAR.

   WHILE CHAR c; read(c); c /= "." DO write(c) OD

Quite commonly, the whole of the material to be repeated needs to come before the test for continuation, leaving nothing to be done between DO and OD. The vacancy must then be filled by the dummy unit SKIP, which does nothing, as shown in the following loop.

   CHAR c;
   WHILE read(c); c = " " DO SKIP OD

This loop reads in a stream of characters until the first non-space character is met, which it leaves in the variable c.

   To repeat a series a given number of times, the usual method is

   TO   *unit*   DO   *series*   OD

The *unit*, which must yield an integer result, is obeyed once at the beginning. Thus, to write 5 spaces, the loop

   TO 5 DO write(space) OD

can be used. When this is obeyed, there is a hidden counter going from 1 to 5. This can be brought out into the open as an object of mode INT, and given an identifier, by writing 'FOR *identifier*' as the start of the clause. The identifier needs no other declaration. Thus,

   INT factorial := 1;
   FOR i TO n DO factorial TIMESAB i OD

puts the product of the first n positive integers in 'factorial'. If n is 0, the DO part is not obeyed at all, and factorial then still holds 1. In this example, the counter might just as well have started from 2, which can be done by writing

   FOR i FROM 2 TO n DO factorial TIMESAB i OD

There are, in fact, five optional parts which can be used to control a loop. They must be given in the order shown below (none, any or all) and appear before the DO part.

Optional Parts in Preamble of a Loop

	mode required	*when obeyed*	*default value*
FOR *identifier*			
FROM *unit1*	INT	once at outset	1
BY *unit2*	INT	once at outset	1
TO *unit3*	INT	once at outset	infinity
WHILE *series*	BOOL	each time	TRUE

The loop counter, the *identifier*, starts with the value of *unit1* and proceeds by increments of *unit2*, which can be positive or negative. Repetition ceases as soon as the counter would pass outside the interval *unit1* to *unit3* (inclusive), or when the series after WHILE first delivers FALSE, whichever happens first.

The loop counter is local to the loop: it can be used in the series after WHILE and the series between DO and OD, though not in the units after FROM, BY and TO. Having mode INT, it cannot receive any assignments. A mistake often made by beginners is to attempt to *declare* the loop counter as a variable.

```
INT i;
FOR i . . . . . . . . OD
```

The two i's here are entirely distinct objects. The first is an ordinary integer variable which becomes inaccessible in the loop clause because the loop counter uses the same identifier. It is worth reiterating that the loop counter is introduced by the word FOR, and that its mode is INT, not REF INT.

As the loop counter disappears when the loop clause has been finished, it cannot be used subsequently to find out how many repetitions were performed. Within the loop its value would have to be assigned to some externally declared variable. Sometimes it is more convenient to go without the loop counter and use the external variable for counting, as in the following episode. This reads in a character stream up to the first non-space character, and puts the count of spaces in the variable n.

```
INT n := 0;
WHILE CHAR c; read(c); c = " "
DO n PLUSAB 1 OD
```

Loops can of course be nested, with an inner loop being part of the series repeated. This is shown in the step given below—which is all one unit. It reads a stream of text and copies out the first six sentences on separate lines.

```
TO 6 DO
        WHILE CHAR c; read(c); c /="."
        DO write(c) OD;
        write((".", newline))
      OD
```

Notice that a bracketed list of items can be given as the parameter of 'write'. This useful construction avoids repeated calls of the procedure.

The lifetime of any space generated in a loop by means of a local generator corresponds with the range of the most recent local declaration. The introduction of a loop counter by 'FOR' does not count as a declaration for this purpose. If there is a local declaration anywhere in the loop clause, locally generated space is lost and regenerated each time round the loop. If there is no such declaration, more and more space will be generated. (An example of this can be found in Section 6.5.)

3.4 Choice

3.4.1 The conditional clause

A conditional clause chooses one result or course of action out of two possible, depending on whether some boolean condition is TRUE or FALSE when evaluated. The standard form of conditional clause is

IF *series* THEN *series* ELSE *series* FI

If the series after IF delivers TRUE, that after THEN will be obeyed, otherwise that after ELSE. Although series are permitted in all three positions, the use of smaller constructions is not precluded. Most commonly, the condition is simply a boolean variable or formula.

For example, to find the colour at some given position on a plan, the following conditional might be used.

IF x > x0 AND x < x1 AND y > y0 AND y < y1
THEN blue
ELSE white
FI

If the result of the boolean formula were needed more than once, it could be held in a variable, thus

BOOL inside : = x > x0 AND x < x1 AND y > y0 AND y < y1;
INT ink : = IF inside THEN blue ELSE white FI

It is always advisable to check the priorities of operators in boolean formulae or use parentheses when in doubt. Programmers unused to boolean variables or constants are often tempted to indulge in (harmless) superfluous writing, such as

BOOL b : = IF i = 1 THEN TRUE ELSE FALSE FI;
IF b = TRUE THEN . . . . FI

which are ill-considered ways of expressing the following

BOOL b : = (i = 1);
IF b THEN . . . . FI

The brackets around $i = 1$ are not actually necessary, as an assignment symbol binds less tightly than any operator in a formula. (Remember that $i = 1$ is a boolean formula.) Similarly, the brackets could be omitted in the identity declaration

BOOL both zero = (i = 0) AND (j = 0)

though the meaning is clearer when they are present, and they cost nothing. They are unnecessary for two reasons. The first equals sign is part of the identity declaration, and is not an operator. Like the assignment symbol, it binds less tightly than any operator. And within the formula on the right, the terms would group in the same way without any brackets, as the priority of the equals operator is 4 whilst that of AND is 3 (see 2.3.2 or refer to Appendix 3 for a complete list).

Conditionals can be used for choosing between taking some course of action and taking no action at all. To save writing SKIP in one of the branches, the short form

IF   *series*   THEN   *series*   FI

can be used. The condition must, of course, be FALSE for nothing to happen. In RS systems, this form should not ordinarily be used if a result is required, as a fault would then occur if the condition were FALSE.

Choosing between more than two courses of action can be expressed in various ways. If the choice can be made by means of an integer, a CASE-clause should be used (3.4.2). Otherwise, IF-clauses can be nested. This is shown in principle by

```
IF condition1
THEN course1
ELSE IF condition2
        THEN course2
        ELSE IF condition3
                THEN course3
                ELSE some other course
                FI
        FI
FI
```

Fortunately, this can be abbreviated to

```
IF condition1 THEN course1
ELIF condition2 THEN course2
ELIF condition3 THEN course3
ELSE some other course
FI
```

The final ELSE part is optional, and there is only one FI. Any depth is permitted.

For very short conditionals, particularly for delivering a result, a contracted notation is preferred by many programmers. Others consider it unintelligible. The notation is shown in

(n < 4 ! 1 !: n < 7 ! 2 ! 3)

The brackets stand for IF and FI, the exclamation marks for THEN or ELSE, and exclamation mark colon (with no intervening space) stands for ELIF. The meaning is therefore

```
IF n < 4 THEN 1
ELIF n < 7 THEN 2
ELSE 3
FI
```

As an enclosed clause, a conditional defines ranges for local declarations. Anything declared between IF and THEN has a range which extends throughout the entire clause, but anything declared after THEN or ELSE is local to its own series.

When a conditional delivers a result, it is good practice to ensure that the last unit in the series after THEN yields a result of the same mode as the last unit of the series after ELSE. Either of these might be the result of the conditional, and if their modes are widely different, there may be a coercion problem (see 3.4.3). Conditionals which deliver results can, of course, be used as primaries in formulae.

3.4.2 The CASE clause

To choose a result or course of action by means of an integer, a CASE clause is used. The choice can be from any number of possibilities. A simple example would be

```
CASE n IN
            31,  IF leap THEN 29 ELSE 28 FI,  31,
            30,  31,  30,  31,  31,  30,  31,  30,  31
ESAC
```

The general form is

```
CASE series
IN   unit , unit ,  . . . , unit
OUT   series
ESAC
```

The *series* after CASE must deliver an integer, and the corresponding *unit* (counted as 1, 2, 3 etc.) is then obeyed. If the integer is less than 1 or greater than the number of units given, the series after OUT is obeyed. The OUT part is optional, but in RS systems a fault occurs if it is absent when it would have been selected.

When a CASE clause is used for choosing a course of action, there may be cases in which no action is required; such units can be written as SKIP, which does nothing. However, when the context requires a result, SKIP would not normally be used, as the value it provides has no meaning. All the units in a CASE clause (and the series in the OUT part) should give results of the same or closely related modes. They will in fact be coerced to the same mode by balancing (3.4.3).

When the selecting integer can be grouped into separate ranges, such as

```
n        101   102   103   201   202  other
result    a     b     c     d     e    f
```

a nested CASE construction can be used, thus

```
CASE n − 100
IN a, b, c
OUT CASE n − 200
       IN d, e
       OUT f
       ESAC
ESAC
```

An abbreviation similar to that in a nested IF-clause permits one to write

CASE n − 100 IN a, b, c
OUSE n − 200 IN d, e
OUT f
ESAC

Each elision of OUT with CASE to form 'OUSE' removes the need for one ESAC at the end.

The same contracted notation is allowed for the CASE clause as for the ordinary conditional clause, with parentheses standing now for CASE and ESAC, exclamation marks for IN and OUT, and exclamation mark colon standing for OUSE. The above example could therefore be contracted to

(n − 100 ! a, b, c !: n − 200 ! d, e ! f)

The range of any identifier or other entity declared between CASE and IN extends over the entire clause, and the range of anything declared after OUT is the OUT part alone.

3.4.3 Balancing the modes

The mode of the result of a conditional or CASE clause cannot depend on the route which the program will take. Both branches of a conditional must yield results of the same mode, and similarly all branches of a CASE clause. If the clause is in a strong context, the results obtained down each branch are separately coerced to the known required mode. For example, the conditional in

REAL y : = IF u THEN x ELSE 0 FI

is in a strong REAL context, so the real variable x will be dereferenced and the integer 0 will be widened to REAL. These coercions are, of course, no different from those which would occur in the absence of the conditional—that is, REAL y := x, or REAL y := 0.

When the context is not strong, the situation is more delicate, for there is no definite mode to aim at. The minimum degree of coercion required to equalize ('balance') the modes is first applied. When a common mode has been reached, any further coercion demanded by the context takes place in the same way as usual. As an example of balancing, consider the conditional

IF u THEN x ELSE i FI

in, say, an operand position. Assume the modes of u, x and i to be BOOL, REF REAL and REF INT respectively. The effect of balancing is to dereference x and i, and then widen the INT to REAL. In a formula, therefore, the operator definition applying to a REAL operand would be selected, even if u were FALSE. Balancing takes place first. Notice also that this conditional could not be used as the left-hand side of an assignment. For example,

IF u THEN x ELSE i FI : = 0   ???

would be wrong, because balancing takes place first, and makes the left-hand side have mode REAL. However, an assignment such as

IF u THEN x ELSE xx FI := 0.0

is acceptable with x having mode REF REAL and xx having mode REF REF REAL. Balancing causes xx to be dereferenced once, and the mode of the conditional is then REF REAL.

In cases of doubt or difficulty, a conditional or case clause can always be cast into a strong position by writing the required mode immediately in front of IF or CASE. This costs nothing and may make the program clearer, but remember that casting cannot bring about any mode changes beyond those for which coercions exist (Appendix 2).

3.5 Jumping

It is universally accepted that jumping from place to place in a program is a bad thing. It obscures the meaning of the program by failing to express any coherent structure. Much of the temptation to jump can be traced back to the use of flow diagrams and to early languages with inadequate control facilities. Procedures, conditionals and loops, especially with WHILE, largely obviate the need for jumps and should always be tried first.

A jump is a unit of the form GOTO *label*. (In RS systems, all jumps must start with the word GOTO, or alternatively with the two words GO TO.) The label marks some place in a series. It must be set in front of a unit in the series, and separated from it by a colon. The form of a label is the same as that of an identifier, and it must be distinct from any identifiers declared in the same series. Any unit in the series can be labelled, provided that there are no declarations later in that series, but labels cannot be set in the series between IF and THEN, CASE and IN, or WHILE and DO, which are technically known as 'enquiry clauses'. The range of a label is the series in which it is set, which makes it impossible to jump *into* any enclosed clause, or between different branches of a conditional. Jumps can be backwards or forwards, but not so as to by-pass any declaration.

One of the less objectionable uses of GOTO is to jump ahead to the final section of a program, possibly from several different places:

```
            IF . . . THEN GOTO epilogue FI;
                . . .
epilogue:   write((newline, result, newline));
            etc etc
END
FINISH
```

Another valid use of GOTO is escape from transput 'event procedures'. These are explained in Section 7.6, and an example of such an escape will be found in Section 7.6.2.

A jump never produces a result and it can occupy any strong context, whether a result is expected or not. With one exception, the jump is simply obeyed when encountered, as for example when i is zero in

    x := CASE i IN a, b, c OUT GOTO lab ESAC

The exception to immediate jumping is a strong context expecting a procedure without parameters. In such a position, a jump is treated as a procedure, as shown at the end of Section 5.4.4.

4 Arrays

4.1 Numbered sequences

Although computing is usually concerned with processing sets of objects, all items of the set are not necessarily wanted at the same time. It is always worth considering whether a program can do its work by some method which reads items in one by one, finishing with each one before reading the next. The mean value of a sequence of numbers can be found in this way, as can many other statistical properties. But when such techniques are inconvenient or impossible, whole sets of the objects required for the computation can—within limits set by practical considerations—be held as *arrays*. All the objects in one array must have the same mode.

The characteristic feature of an array is that its elements are in a numbered sequence. For example, height above sea level at regular intervals along a railway track could be held as an array of reals, and by means of an integer n, which could be computed in the program, the nth height could be picked out. If the survey points were at irregular distances along the line, the sequence could still be numbered, but the distances as well as the heights would then be needed. An array of mode

    [ ]STRUCT(REAL distance, height)

might be used. To take another example, the depth of the sea at points on a rectangular grid could be held as an array of reals, but two integers would be needed to locate one element in a convenient way. Integers used for this purpose are known as array *subscripts*, and the act of attaching subscripts to an array to define a particular element is known as *indexing* the array. The number of subscripts required is the dimensionality of the array, and arrays with one dimension are called *rows*.

Indexing is subject to an important and obvious limitation well known to every experienced programmer. As all arrays are finite in size, the range of values for any subscript is bounded. For each dimension there is a lower and upper bound beyond which the subscript must not go. The number of elements in a row is given by

    upper bound − lower bound + 1

and for multi-dimensional arrays by a product of this sum over each dimension. If the lower bound of a row is 1, the upper bound is just the number of elements, and in this chapter such rows are called 'simple rows' and are considered first. This helps to keep the account free from extraneous detail, as arrays with lower bound 1 can be handled more simply than others.

4.2 Simple rows (lower bound 1)

4.2.1 Declaration

The declaration of a variable v for a simple row of n reals is

[n]REAL v

This consists of three parts,

[ ]REAL	the mode of the array for which space is required
n	the number of elements
v	identifier for the variable (mode REF[ ]REAL)

Arrays are objects whose space requirements are not completely determined by their mode alone. The mode of an array does not include the number of elements, but in a variable declaration for an array, the size must be inserted in the initial pair of square brackets. For a simple one-dimensional array, it can be written as a unit delivering an integer result which will be computed when the declaration is obeyed.

The elements of an array can have any mode, and may therefore involve other arrays. If the mode written in the array variable declaration contains further pairs of square brackets, these must give sizes if, and only if, such sizes are relevant to the immediate space requirements. Notice, for instance, that the second pair of brackets in

[n]REF[ ]REAL w

is empty. This declaration has to make space for n references to other rows, which are not being declared here. Sizes are never required after the word REF. A different situation is that in

[n][m]REAL y

Here both sizes are needed. The reasoning is as follows. The declaration has to make space for the n elements of a row. It cannot do this unless the sizes of the elements are known. As each element is a row of reals, the sizes of these rows must be given. Exactly the same argument applies to the declaration

[n]STRUCT(INT i, [m]REAL r)s

Space is needed for n elements, each of which is one integer and a row of reals. As the row of reals is part of the element, its size must be given. The total space required for s is that for n integers and n*m reals.

A row variable can acquire its initial values in various ways, element by element (4.2.2) or all at once. If the data is to be read in, all the elements can be read in together. (The elements in this case must not be or contain any references, for these have no existence outside the program.) A common pattern for reading in an array, given suitably arranged data, is

```
INT n;
read(n);
[n]REAL v;
read(v)
```

There is no need for a loop, as read(v) inputs all the elements. A less usual way of giving values to a row variable is by a single assignment, as in

[n]REAL v1 : = v

This causes all the elements of v to be copied into v1. Both sides must have the same subscript bounds. The facility is noteworthy, though not frequently used. Equally unusual in practice is assignment from a collateral display, such as

[4]REAL z : = (0.0, 0.0, 0.0, 0.0)

Obviously this is a method which can be used only if the size of the array is known when the program is written, and even then it is inconvenient for large rows. For 'clearing' an array variable to noughts (or whatever constants are appropriate for the mode of the elements), particular systems will normally offer some special facility such as a library operator. These, then, are the available methods of filling a row variable in one step. The method of assigning values to elements one by one is described in Section 4.2.2.

Constant rows can be declared by identity declarations such as

[ ]INT vesuvius = (1, 2, 3, 4, 3, 2, 1);
[ ]STRUCT(INT sides, REAL minutes)siegfried
    = ((3, 82.3), (3, 74.3), (4, 80.8));
[ ][ ]INT farey = ((0, 1), (1, 3), (1, 2), (2, 3), (1, 1))

In the first of these examples, the row has 7 elements. As the lower bound of a row display is taken to be 1, the lower bound of vesuvius is 1 and its upper bound is 7. The second example shows a row display of structure displays (as we can see from the mode), whilst the third shows a row display of row displays. No sizes are included in the left-hand sides, as identity declarations—unlike variable declarations—do not create working space. The identifiers simply stand for the rows actually given. These need not be expressed as collateral displays, but there is little point in using array identity declarations to 'snapshot' existing array variables, for in RS systems an array identity declaration does not cause a new copy of the array to be made.

4.2.2 Indexing

To pick out one element of a row, a subscript must be used. In mathematics, subscripts are written below the line, but in programming languages such as Algol 68 they are written in square brackets after the row. The individual elements of 'vesuvius' (previous section) are

vesuvius[1] . . . . . . vesuvius[7]

As the mode of vesuvius is [ ]INT, each of these elements has mode INT. Similarly, the individual elements of 'farey' are

farey[1] . . . . farey[5]

and each of these has mode [ ]INT. To pick out the first element of farey[4], i.e. the first of the row (2, 3), a further subscript can be supplied,

farey[4][1]

and this element has mode INT.

When a row *variable* is subscripted, the result is a *variable*. The REF is transmitted to the element. Take, for instance, the row variable declared by

[3]INT rowvar

The complete variable 'rowvar' has mode REF[ ]INT, and the mode of rowvar[1] is REF INT. This makes it possible to assign values to individual elements, as in

rowvar[1] : = vesuvius[4];
rowvar[2] : = vesuvius[5];
rowvar[3] : = vesuvius[6]

The syntactic form of an indexed row is

primary [*unit*]

The *primary* must deliver a row or reference to a row. If there are any further REFs, they are removed by dereferencing. The subscript is a *unit* which must deliver an integer, and the whole construction is classed as a primary.

Subscripting and looping very frequently go hand in hand, as in the following loop which abbreviates the previous assignments:

FOR i TO 3 DO rowvar[i] : = vesuvius[i + 3] OD

(A shorter method still is given in Section 4.2.3.) When running through all the elements of a row, it is essential not to go over the top, but there is no need to refer back to the row declaration to make sure of the upper bound. The operator UPB applied to the row (or row variable) delivers it. The habit of writing

FOR i TO UPB row DO . . .

has prevented many a program from coming to grief while running. The corresponding lower bound operator LWB is not required if, as assumed throughout this section, the lower bound is known to be 1.

4.2.3 Trimming

As well as selecting a single element from an array, it is possible to select a subset of the elements. This is called 'trimming' the array. In simple cases, a trimmer is a pair of integers separated by a colon and used in square brackets instead of a subscript. Thus, if 'vesuvius' is a row of 7 integers, vesuvius[4 : 6] is a subset consisting of the elements from 4 to 6 inclusive. The subset is a simple row having its own lower bound of 1.

A previous example showed the assignment of vesuvius[4], vesuvius[5] and vesuvius[6] to the integer row variable 'rowvar', declared to be of size 3. The loop previously shown,

    FOR i TO 3 DO rowvar[i] : = vesuvius[i + 3] OD

can now be replaced by a single assignment

    rowvar : = vesuvius[4 : 6]

This shows the trimming of a constant row. Variable rows can also be trimmed, as follows.

    [100]INT h;
    h[2 : 4] : = (10, 100, 1000)

This puts 10, 100 and 1000 into h[2], h[3] and h[4] respectively. The other elements of h are not touched. Remember that, whenever a row is assigned to a row variable, their sizes must agree and so must their actual bounds. In the last example, the lower bound on the left is 1 because a trimmed row variable is defined to have lower bound 1, and the lower bound on the right is 1 because the same is true of a collateral row display.

    If one of the integers in a trimmer is omitted, it is assumed to be one of the bounds of the original row. For example,

    [7][3]CHAR days;
    days[: 3] : = ("mon", "tue", "wed");
    days[4 :] : = ("thu", "fri", "sat", "sun")

Such a use of blanks is not just an obtuse form of laziness. Inside a procedure, the bounds of an array passed in as a parameter may not be known. It is then not unreasonable to write d[4 :] rather than the equally correct d[4 : UPB d].

    The act of putting subscripts or trimmers in square brackets after an array is termed *slicing*. A row or row variable can be sliced and sliced again. Thus

    h[21 : 30][4 : 7][2]

is actually h[25]. Repeated slicing can occur in a natural way when a subset of an array is passed to a procedure which then slices it further.

    The syntactic form of a trimmed row is

    primary [*unit* : *unit*]

If the mode of the *primary* begins with more than one REF, it is dereferenced to a single REF, which is transmitted to the slice. The two *units* must deliver integers, and the construction as a whole is classed as a primary.

4.3 More general arrays

4.3.1 Two or more dimensions
Multi-dimensional arrays should always be carefully sized up when a program is at the planning stage, as they can easily demand more space than is available. In

scientific projects, computers used for three-dimensional modelling in fields such as meteorology or aerodynamics have to be substantially larger than those needed for work in one or two dimensions.

In this section two-dimensional arrays are used for illustration; generalization to three or more dimensions is obvious and straightforward. Within the square brackets associated with arrays, whether for declarations or other uses, each dimension is taken in turn with commas for separation. Thus, to declare and input to a two-dimensional array variable of mode REF[,]REAL, we write

```
[50, 10]REAL depths;
read(depths)
```

This reads in 500 numbers. If the numbers are set out (in the data stream) on 50 lines with 10 numbers on each line, the reading order will correspond to the 50 by 10 'row-row' declared. Visually, the data would appear as 50 rows and 10 columns, and for those who prefer to think in this way, it is useful to remember that the number of rows comes first, columns second, when writing a declaration. In Algol 68, the mathematicians' convention of 'rows before columns' always applies in two-dimensional work.

To output the array with this same layout, formatted output (Section 7.5) would normally be used to ensure tidy spacing of the numbers in each line and possibly to take a blank line after every ten lines of numbers. Without formatting, the new lines can be produced by

```
FOR i TO 50
DO FOR j TO 10
    DO write(depths[i, j]) OD;
    write(newline)
OD
```

This shows the use of two subscripts, which select the element in the ith row and jth column of depths. If one subscript is given and the other left blank, a two-dimensional array is sliced to one dimension. The ith row of depths is depths[i,] and the jth column is depths[, j]. This can be used to shorten the above example by outputting whole rows together.

```
FOR i TO 50
DO write((depths[i, ], newline)) OD
```

The 50 could have been written as '1 UPB depths', which uses the dyadic form of the operator UPB. The left operand is an integer to indicate which of the upper bounds is required (1 for that of the first dimension, 2 for the second, etc.). The 50 could also have been written as 'UPB depths', using the monadic form of UPB, as this always applies to the first or the only dimension of an array.

When, in any piece of program, an array appears several times over with the same subscript(s), there is an opportunity to reduce the overheads associated with indexing. In the following episode, a two-dimensional integer array h is inspected element by element in order to count up the number of negative values.

```
INT negcount := 0;
FOR i TO UPB h
DO FOR j TO 2 UPB h
   DO IF h[i, j] < 0
      THEN negcount +:= 1
      FI
   OD
OD
```

In the inner loop, the array is repeatedly indexed with the same value of i while the other index, j, progresses from 1 to its upper bound. This is unnecessary work which can be avoided as follows.

```
INT negcount := 0;
FOR i TO UPB h
DO [ ]INT hi = h[i, ];
   FOR j TO UPB hi
   DO IF hi[j] < 0
      THEN negcount +:= 1
      FI
   OD
OD
```

Such an optimization might be carried a stage further if there were repeated occurrences of hi[j] in the inner loop. The declaration 'INT hij = hi[j] could be introduced to avoid all but one indexing of hi. Finally, it should be clear that if h were an array *variable* (mode REF[ ]INT), the identity declaration

REF[ ]INT hi = h[i,]

would be just as effective as the one shown in the example, and would make assignments to hi[j] possible. Such assignments would, of course, be the same as assignments to h[i, j], for they are both exactly the same reference.

Collateral assignment to a two-dimensional array involves a row display of row displays, as in

```
[4, 4]INT magic square := ((16,  3,  2, 13),
                           ( 5, 10, 11,  8),
                           ( 9,  6,  7, 12),
                           ( 4, 15, 14,  1))
```

When using nested collaterals, it is useful to remember that the order of subscripting corresponds to taking the outer level first. Thus, magic square[2, 1] is the integer 5. Two-dimensional arrays can, of course, be trimmed in either or both dimensions, so

magic square[4, 2 : 3]

is the one-dimensional subset whose elements are the integers 15 and 14. As explained in the section on trimming (4.2.3), the bounds of this subset are 1:2.

4.3.2 The rowing coercion

In a strong context which demands a [ ]INT, say, it is permitted to supply an INT, which will be converted into a row of just a single element. This is the *rowing coercion*. One of its uses is illustrated in the first line of

[ ]INT b0 = 1,
        b2 = (1, 2, 1),
        b4 = (1, 4, 6, 4, 1)

The value of b0 cannot be expressed as a row display, as there is no such thing as a collateral with a single item. Brackets round the 1 would be ineffective, for the mode of 1 is INT whether or not it is bracketed. The rowing coercion obviates this difficulty.

Rowing can also increase the number of dimensions of an array by 1, as in

[,]REAL mu = (1.0, 1.0, 1.0)

or in

[1, 3]REAL xu : = (1.0, 1.0, 1.0)

The strong row-row of real contexts on the right-hand sides of these declarations cause the collateral displays to be treated as two-dimensional arrays of size 1 in the first dimension and 3 in the second. The rowing coercion always adds its extra dimension at the *front* of the mode. The initialization in

[3, 1]REAL yu : = (1.0, 1.0, 1.0)   ???

is therefore wrong. To declare such an array variable and fill the array with 1's, the two steps

[3, 1]REAL yu;
yu[, 1] : = (1.0, 1.0, 1.0)

could be used. The mode required for the right-hand side of this assignment is simply [ ]REAL, and no rowing is called for.

Rowing will convert a row to a 'row-row' mode ([,] . . .) or to a 'row of row' mode ([ ][ ] . . .), according to the requirements of the context. It will work through single references if necessary, converting REF REAL for example to REF[ ]REAL. And it will be applied repeatedly if required. The effect of rowing can be summarized as the introduction of 'row-' or 'row of' at the front of any mode, or after its first REF.

4.3.3 Lower bounds not 1

Adherence to the preferred lower bound of 1 is not always convenient. The items input to a row variable may have some actual or implied numbering in the outside world, not starting at 1. To declare an array variable with any bounds, the size information has to be given differently. Instead of a single integer, two integers are given in the form

    lower bound : *upper bound*

These bounds can be given as any units which will deliver integers. If the bounds are equal, the row will contain just one element—from which we see that a row containing no elements would have an upper bound one less than the lower bound. This is not a wholly absurd occurrence, and does not give rise to a fault.

As an example of the construction, the array variable 'map', declared by

> [−3:3, −2:2]INT map

could be used to hold a rectangular lattice of integers with map[0, 0] as the central element. The 35 values could be input in one step by 'read(map)'. Collateral assignments in the program need more care. Thus

> map[0,] := (0, 0, 0, 0, 0)   ???

is a wrong way of putting zeros in the centre row of the array, because the bounds of the unsubscripted dimension are still −2:2. The bounds of the row display on the right-hand side are 1:5. This disagreement is not allowed, and there are various ways of remedying it. Using a technique already described,

> map[0, −2:2] := (0, 0, 0, 0, 0)

is correct, as trimming always gives a lower bound of 1. The slice taken here is the whole range of the second dimension. Somewhat obscurely, therefore, we are allowed to write

> map[0, :] := (0, 0, 0, 0, 0)

because the integers omitted from a trimmer are taken to be bounds of the full array. But a better plan, stylistically, is to use 'AT':

> map[0, AT 1] := (0, 0, 0, 0, 0)

The construction

> AT *new lower bound*

can be used in any subscript position which would otherwise be blank, or after any trimmer, to shift the subscripting range to a new lower bound. The new bound can be expressed as any unit which will deliver an integer. As a further example,

> REF[,]INT kernel = map[−2:2 AT −2, −1:1 AT −1]

defines 'kernel' as the subset of 'map' obtained by leaving out all the elements round the edge whilst maintaining the original subscript positions. Thus the bounds of 'kernel' are −2:2 and −1:1, and its central element, kernel[0,0], is map[0,0].

In all the examples given of collateral assignment, the bounds of the array have been shifted to suit the collateral. Though perhaps clumsier, it is possible to shift the bounds of the display instead, by writing

> map[0,] := [ ]INT(0, 0, 0, 0, 0)[AT −2]

The point to notice here is that a collateral cannot itself be sliced until it has been cast as a row display; the position before an indexer is not strong, and this position has to be considered before any larger context can be taken into account.

4.3.4 Flexible arrays

Once an array variable has been declared, space for its elements is reserved, and cannot be extended to hold more. But an entirely fresh allocation of space can be obtained if a special mode is used. A variable with this property is called a flexible array variable, and its mode has FLEX before the square brackets. The fresh space is allocated whenever a *whole array* is assigned to the array variable; the bounds then change to those of the new array. Flexibility can apply to array variables of any number of dimensions, but the number of dimensions itself can never be changed throughout the life of the variable.

As an example, the variable declaration

FLEX[3]INT f

declares f to have an initial size of 3, and mode REF FLEX[ ]INT. Individual assignments to f[1], f[2] and f[3] can be made in the usual way, and any attempt to extend the variable by using f[4] would be illegal, just as it is for an ordinary array. The subscript would be out of bounds. However, the collateral assignment

f := (5, 4, 3, 2, 1)

creates new space and effectively makes f into a new variable. The new size may be greater or less than it was previously, and can be made zero by assigning a collateral display containing no elements (a so-called 'vacuum'), thus

f := ( )

After this assignment, the lower bound of f is 1 and the upper bound is 0. Flexible array variables are often declared with size 0 in the first instance, unless some particular size is needed from the outset.

The most useful purpose served by a flexible array variable is to accommodate an array of unpredictable size produced as the result of some operator or procedure. By the time the result is delivered, it is too late to declare a variable of corresponding size, but it can be assigned immediately to a flexible array variable. Thus, if p is a procedure which delivers a row of integers, this can be assigned to f, without regard to size, by

f := p

Without using a flexible array, the alternative would be

[ ]INT result = p;
[UPB result]INT v := result

—hardly an elegant solution to the problem.

Despite the usual terminology 'flexible array', the property of flexibility actually belongs to array references, not to arrays themselves. There is no such thing as a flexible array constant. Flexible array references can occur within any other modes, for example as elements of a constant row:

FLEX[0]CHAR s1, s2, s3, s4;
[ ]REF FLEX[ ]CHAR names = (s1, s2, s3, s4)

Flexible arrays can also be elements of a row variable which is not itself flexible, such as

   [n]FLEX[0]REAL rf

Here, each of the elements of rf has the mode REF FLEX[ ]REAL, and rows of unpredictable and different sizes could be assigned to all the rf[i]. An example of a flexible array as a field of a structure variable is

   STRUCT(INT type, FLEX[0, 0]REAL sizes)pad

When the 'sizes' field is selected (6.2.1), its mode REF FLEX[,]REAL is that of a flexible array variable.

   Flexible array references introduce a new note into the language, for up to now an identifier has always stood for the same object throughout its lifetime. Thus, a real variable may refer to one number and then another, and the reference itself never changes. But when an array is assigned to a flexible array variable, the *reference itself changes*—because new space has to be found. This fact carries with it a drawback concerning any references which may have been derived from the original flexible reference, such as references to slices of the original array. These must not be held for later use, because they do *not* change when the original flexible reference changes and they may therefore become invalid. Derived references can arise not only from slicing, but also from the rowing coercion and (to anticipate Chapter 6) from field selection applied to a flexible array variable whose elements are structures. Such derived references can safely be used on the left of assignments, but must not themselves be assigned, identified or delivered as results. Many programmers prefer to avoid flexible arrays and adopt alternative methods. This is always possible with the use of an additional REF. For example, if the procedure p mentioned above had delivered a reference to the row of integers instead of the actual row, the result could have been assigned to an ordinary variable of mode REF REF[ ]INT. However, one field of application in which flexible arrays are normally used in a straightforward way is that of character string handling, and to this we now turn.

4.4 Character strings

Although there is no difference of principle between characters and any other objects, characters tend to occur mainly in sequences. By the facilities it provides, Algol 68 recognizes this fact and aims at an efficient match between the needs of users and the capabilities of machines, This is especially true in RS systems, as explained in Section 4.4.1.

   For work with characters, the collateral is a clumsy form of display, as may easily be seen:

   [ ]CHAR name = ("P", "i", "c", "a", "s", "s", "o")

A more natural representation is the continuous string in quotes, thus

   [ ]CHAR name = "Picasso"

Any of the characters defined as objects of mode CHAR for the computer system in use can be included in a string, and this may include upper and lower case alphabets. A special arrangement has to apply for a quote character if this is needed within the string; it is represented by a *pair* of quote symbols. A string must not stretch over more than one line, but two strings separated only by spaces or new lines are taken to be parts of one long string. (Such parts of strings must not, of course, be contiguous.) The following is an example of one long string:

"Some of the jury wrote it down ""important"","
" and some ""unimportant"".   Alice could see"
" this, as she was near enough to look over"
" their slates; ""but it doesnt matter a bit"""
", she thought to herself."

Strings can be handled in a program as objects of mode [ ]CHAR, but variables of mode REF[ ]CHAR are often unsuitable as the number of characters must be given in the declaration. The most convenient variables for character strings are flexible ones of mode REF FLEX[ ]CHAR. There is in fact a standard Algol 68 mode STRING, defined as

MODE STRING   =   FLEX[0]CHAR

Being flexible, STRING variables will accept strings of any length.

STRING s : = "damsel";
s : = "a damsel with a dulcimer";
s : = ""

The lower bound of s remains as 1 throughout these assignments, as it would for collateral displays. The upper bound is 6 after the first assignment, 24 after the second and 0 after the third. The upper bound of a STRING variable can also change as a result of an input; 'read(s)' reads characters from the input data stream up to the end of the current line (or sooner, if a terminating character has been set as described in Chapter 7).

The mode STRING need not be confined to variable declarations. It can be employed in identity declarations for string constants, such as

STRING duchy = "Cornwall"

As this declaration does not introduce a reference, FLEX cannot apply, so STRING is interpreted simply as [ ]CHAR.

4.4.1 Modes of strings in RS systems

In RS systems, string denotations do not, a priori, have mode [ ]CHAR. They have modes which are special to RS systems and which embody their actual length. Examples of these character structures are shown in the identity declarations

STRUCT 4 CHAR date = "1984";
STRUCT 3 CHAR country = "USA"

The integers 4 and 3 are part of the modes, and must be expressed as actual integer denotations. These modes are implemented with minimal overheads, and in work involving large numbers of short fixed length strings they are far more economical than arrays. Economy is the intention underlying the Algol 68 mode BYTES, which corresponds to a machine-dependent number of characters, usually 4. In RS systems, BYTES is defined as a character structure. For ICL 2900 systems, for instance, the mode BYTES is defined as

MODE BYTES = STRUCT 4 CHAR

Character structures can be indexed like rows of characters having lower bound 1. Consequently, in any RS system, objects of mode BYTES can be indexed like rows. (A subset formed by trimming behaves as an object of mode [ ]CHAR.)

    If it is important to adhere strictly to the standard form of Algol 68, character structures need not appear explicitly in any program. Although implicit as the *a priori* modes of strings, character structures are coercible to [ ]CHAR in strong positions and in operand positions.

5 Procedures

5.1 Introduction

Procedures are the means by which given pieces of program can be obeyed on demand in any number of different contexts. To prepare a piece of program for such use, it is written out as a 'routine text' and given an identifier by an identity declaration. Subsequently, whenever the identifier is used in the correct way—known as a procedure call—the routine text is obeyed. Certain procedures considered to be of general importance have been defined and given identifiers by the Algol 68 system itself. These procedures can be called at any time; no declarations by the user are required.

Programmers should never hesitate to define their own procedures. It helps greatly with the design process and can prevent large programs from becoming obscured by detail. When faced with a new programming task, it is often a good plan to write and test procedures first. This makes sure that particular detailed methods are feasible and correct, and gives confidence when proceeding to the larger problems. More experienced programmers may prefer to imagine certain procedures already written until they are sure that the larger strategy for solving the problem will actually require their use. Whichever order is adopted, the specifications of procedures are considered at an early stage.

5.2 The call of a procedure

The very first thing to know about a procedure is its mode, for without this, it cannot be correctly called. A procedure mode has the form

> PROC (*mode, mode, . . .*) *mode*

The modes in parentheses describe the objects of data needed by the procedure—its parameters. There may be any number of these, and if there are none, the whole bracketed part of the mode is absent. The final mode, which must always be present, describes the result which the procedure delivers to its context. If it delivers no result, the mode is written as VOID. In Algol 68, this is the only formal distinction made between a procedure which delivers a result like a mathematical function, and one which advances the computation in some other way.

The following examples illustrate the relationship between the mode of a procedure and the task it is required to perform. These are all simple cases of procedures which deliver results. The first two are, in fact, standard procedures which do not have to be declared.

procedure to deliver ...	*mode*
a random real number between 0.0 and 1.0 ('random')	PROC REAL
the real square root of a given real number ('sqrt')	PROC(REAL)REAL
the real area of a triangle, given three positive real numbers as the lengths of the sides ('area', say)	PROC(REAL, REAL, REAL)REAL

Calls of procedures such as these can be used as primaries in formulae, thus

random $*$ area(p, p, p + 2.5) $*$ sqrt(2)

The parameters given in procedure calls must provide values whose modes correspond one-to-one with those appearing in the mode of the procedure. The positions occupied by the parameters are therefore strong, and all necessary coercions are applied. In the above example, if p is a real variable, it will be dereferenced to REAL, which is the mode required for all three of the parameters of 'area'. Similarly, the parameter of 'sqrt' will be widened from the given INT value to the REAL value demanded by the procedure. Parameters can be given in the form of expressions (—units, in fact) and these are evaluated before the procedure itself starts work. Nothing should be assumed about the order in which the various parameters of a procedure will be evaluated. A call such as

area(p := 2.0, p, 1.0)   ???

is wrong—not because one of the parameters is an assignment, but because the second parameter might be evaluated before or after the first, with uncertain consequences.

A question often asked by Algol 68 students is whether a procedure can deliver more than one result. It can deliver only one object to the context, but several values could be packaged in one data structure (Chapter 6) and this would then be a single object. Another method of obtaining answers from a procedure is to provide as parameters variables declared earlier in the program. The procedure can assign values to these variables. To illustrate this point, we shall consider the design of a procedure which would answer the following questions.

> Given three positive numbers, could they be the lengths of the sides of a triangle? If so, what would be its area and perimeter?

In choosing an identifier and a mode for the procedure, we should bear in mind how we would most like to write the call. If the possibility of forming a triangle is to be tested in a conditional, it would be convenient if the procedure were to deliver a boolean result. This leads to the following plan.

identifier:	triangle
mode:	PROC(REAL, REAL, REAL, REF REAL, REF REAL) BOOL

The first three parameters would be the given lengths, and the fourth and fifth would be variables to which the procedure would if possible assign the area and perimeter. The boolean result would be TRUE if the lengths could form a triangle and FALSE if not. This procedure could be called in the following manner.

```
REAL a, b, c, area, perim, roundness;
read((a, b, c));
IF triangle(a, b, c, area, perim)
THEN roundness := 4*pi*area/perim**2
ELSE write ("not a triangle")
FI
```

As another exercise in the choice of mode for a procedure, consider the specification of a procedure which would sort the elements of a given row of strings into alphabetical order. In such problems, the original ordering can often be discarded. If so, the procedure can overwrite the data with the answer, which suggests

    identifier: sort
    mode: PROC(REF[ ]STRING)VOID

To show a call of this procedure, the following extract reads in an unknown number of names (less than 100) on separate lines, terminated by a line containing an oblique stroke only. The names are sorted and printed out.

```
[100]STRING names;
INT n;
FOR i TO UPB names
WHILE read((names[i], newline));
        names[i] /= "/"
DO n := i OD;
sort(names[ :n]);
FOR i TO n DO write ((names[i], newline)) OD
```

Comments on the practical use of various types of parameter mode are given in Section 5.4.

The syntax for a procedure call is

    primary (unit , unit , ...)

with one unit for each actual parameter. If there are no parameters at all, the call consists of the primary alone—a case discussed further in Section 5.5. Although the primary is normally the procedure's own identifier, it can be any primary construction that will yield a procedure, possibly after dereferencing. It could, for instance, be a procedure variable (Section 5.7).

5.3 Procedure declarations

The type of declaration almost always used for declaring a procedure is

    PROC *identifier* = *routine-text*

This is a special abbreviated form of identity declaration with PROC instead of the full mode of the procedure. In a full identity declaration, the right-hand side is a unit; in this shorter form, it has to be a *routine text*, a type of unit which defines a procedure by giving its actual text in the form

(*mode id , mode id , ... mode id*) *mode : unit*

where *id* stands for identifier. The part before the colon is the heading which embodies the mode of the procedure and also includes identifiers as *formal parameters*. These are for use only within the routine text itself. The *actual* parameters obviously cannot be used in the definition of the procedure: they are given in its call. If several consecutive formal parameters have the same mode, the mode can be omitted for all but the first of the group, and if the procedure has no parameters, the bracketed part of the heading is omitted altogether. As in the mode of the procedure, the heading concludes with the mode of the result, or VOID if no result is to be delivered.

The unit which follows the heading is the 'procedure body'. It could simply be a formula, but is more usually an enclosed clause such as a conditional or (most commonly of all) a simple closed clause. The result of the procedure is the result of the body, after any coercion which may be required to reach the mode given at the end of the heading. If this is VOID, the result of the body is simply discarded. The body of a procedure is in a strong context.

As an example, the following declares the procedure 'triangle' introduced in the previous section. It includes a specification in English as a comment.

```
PROC triangle = (REAL x, y, z, REF REAL a, p)BOOL:
COMMENT
            The procedure attempts to construct a triangle with sides of
            lengths x, y, z. If successful, it puts the area in a, the perimeter
            in p and delivers the result TRUE. Otherwise it leaves the
            variables a and p undisturbed and delivers FALSE.
COMMENT
BEGIN REAL s = (x + y + z)/2;
        REAL square = s * (s − x) * (s − y) * (s − z);
        BOOL possible = square > 0;
        IF possible THEN a := sqrt(square); p := s * 2 FI;
        possible
END
```

The area of the triangle is calculated by the well known formula involving the semi-perimeter s. If the formula leads to the square root of a negative number, one of the given positive lengths is greater than the sum of the other two and a triangle cannot be formed. The boolean result is then FALSE. Notice how this is given as the final step of the simple closed clause which forms the procedure body.

When a procedure is called, the actual parameters replace the formal parameters. In Algol 68, the way this is done is defined exactly: it is as though the formal parameters were on the left-hand sides of identity declarations and the actual parameters on the right. These implied declarations are the very first things to be obeyed. For an example of this principle, consider a call of 'triangle' such as

triangle(a, b, c, area, perim)

where a, b, c, area and perim are all real variables declared earlier in the program. This call is equivalent to

```
BEGIN
    REAL x = a, y = b, z = c;
    REF REAL a = area, p = perim;
    REAL s = (x + y + z)/2;
    REAL square = s * (s − x) * (s − y) * (s − z);
    BOOL possible = square > 0;
    IF possible THEN a : = sqrt(square); p : = s * 2 FI;
    possible
END
```

This is simply the body of 'triangle', but with the implied declarations for the parameters explicitly written in. It makes it clear that the formal parameter identifiers are local to the routine text, and shows that the actual parameters are evaluated and strongly coerced before the procedure is obeyed.

5.3.1 Use of non-locals

Although a program normally communicates data to a procedure through parameters, the procedure body can in fact use other objects declared in the program if their identifiers are accessible to the routine text. Below is a simple example in the shape of a complete program to calculate compound interest on $100, using the mathematical formula

$$100((1 + rate)**t − 1)$$

where rate is the fractional interest rate per year, and t is the number of years. The calculation is repeated for different rates and times until zero time is input.

```
PROGRAM compound interest
BEGIN REAL percent;
    INT years;
    PROC interest = REAL:
        100.0 * ((1.0 + percent/100.0) ** years − 1.0);
    WHILE read((percent, years)); years > 0
    DO write((interest, newline)) OD
END FINISH
```

Non-local variables used in a routine text, such as 'percent' and 'years', must obviously be valid as identifiers where they appear, but they need not have had any values assigned to them at that stage. The reals held by the variables will not be used until the routine text is obeyed, which is at the procedure call.

When writing a procedure, a choice must be made between passing data through parameters or just using existing non-locals. As a general rule, procedures should be as self-contained as possible. By channelling all communication from the program to the procedure through parameters, the risk of unexpected side-effects is much reduced, for when such a procedure is called, it can only influence its parameters. If the procedure needs working spaces, these should *always* be declared within the routine text, so limiting their range and reducing risk of confusion.

5.3.2 Use of EXIT

To accomplish a task of reasonable size, a routine text must usually include a series of steps. The body of the routine, therefore, will often be a bracketed series or simple closed clause, and when this is the case the last unit obeyed is the one which delivers the result of the procedure. This need not, in fact, be the last of the units as written. There are two methods of effecting an earlier escape. One is to use GOTO *label* as a means of jumping out to some external label. This is not good practice, and it prevents the procedure from delivering any result. A better method is to use the word EXIT in place of a semi-colon at the required point of departure.

In a simple closed clause, EXIT acts like an alternative END to the clause. It must come after one of the main units in the series, because its effect is always to jump to the end of the smallest (i.e. most local) series in which it occurs. Thus, the body of a routine text might take the form

```
BEGIN
      ... ;
      x EXIT
alt:  ... ;
      y
END
```

This simple closed clause delivers x if that step is reached, or delivers y if 'GOTO alt' has been obeyed before then. A moment's reflection shows that the step following an EXIT must be labelled, as otherwise it could never be reached. An exit between two units must in fact adhere to the syntactic form

   unit EXIT *label* : *unit*

As already implied, the word EXIT, unlike a semi-colon, does not void the result of the preceding *unit*.

5.4 Useful parameter modes

The parameters of a procedure can have any modes, and the purpose of the following sub-sections is to comment on the practical use of the main types: simple modes, references, arrays and procedures. No extra rules are introduced; the mechanism of parameter substitution is exactly defined by implicit identity declarations of the form

   mode formal-parameter = actual-parameter

These declarations are not written in the program, but they are obeyed automatically, one for each parameter, before the body of the routine is obeyed. Thus each actual parameter is strongly coerced to the mode written in the heading of the routine text.

5.4.1 Simple modes

A simple mode such as INT, REAL, BOOL or CHAR is used to hand over to a procedure a basic object of data. The procedure can never put such a parameter on the left-hand side of an assignment, as it is not a variable. If a variable is given as the actual parameter, the value to which it refers cannot be changed by the procedure, as dereferencing takes place before anything is handed over.

It must be remembered that although integers can be widened to reals, the converse does not apply. A fault occurs if a REAL is given as an actual parameter when the procedure asks for an INT. The real must be explicitly converted to an integer by means of one of the standard operators ENTIER or ROUND.

5.4.2 References

There are two quite different reasons for using a reference parameter. One is to supply the procedure with a variable, to which it can assign a result. The other is to give it access to some large data structure without handing over the structure itself.

The use of a reference parameter as a receptacle for an answer has been shown in the 'triangle' example (Section 5.2 and 5.3) and little more need be said. Bear in mind that an actual parameter of mode REF INT cannot be supplied if the procedure requires a REF REAL, nor vice versa. Both of these would cause a fault. The only coercion which can alter a reference mode is rowing, which can coerce (say) a REF REAL to REF[ ]REAL.

In order to give a procedure access to some large data structure, the use of a reference should be regarded as normal practice. Suppose that a procedure p requires access to all the data about a particular criminal, as in

> MODE VILLAIN = STRUCT(STRING name, BOOL violent,
>
> $\qquad\qquad$ ... ...
>
> $\qquad\qquad$ REF[ ]VILLAIN partners);
>
> PROC p = (REF VILLAIN v)BOOL: ... ...

Without REF in the mode of the parameter of p, an object of mode VILLAIN would have to be passed across, and this would entail copying the whole structure, which might be very lengthy. With REF, exactly the same data is made accessible to the procedure, but the object copied, being only a reference, is much smaller in size. The procedure now also has the facility of assignment to all or any selected parts of the data structure. The same considerations can apply to the use of array references as to structure references, though in RS systems an array parameter without REF does not entail copying of all the elements.

5.4.3 Arrays

An array is usually passed to a procedure as a variable; this is shown in the following program for counting the zeros in an array.

```
PROGRAM zero count
BEGIN INT n;   read(n);
       [n]INT a;   read(a);
       PROC zeros  =  (REF[ ]INT r)INT:
       BEGIN
           INT z  := 0;
           FOR i TO UPB r
           DO IF r[i] = 0 THEN z PLUSAB 1 FI OD;
           z
       END;
       write((zeros(a), " zeros found"))
END FINISH
```

Notice particularly that the procedure uses the operator UPB to discover the upper bound of the array. This comes as second nature to experienced Algol 68 programmers; it would be poor programming to use the variable n non-locally, even though in this instance it would have the same effect. As written, the procedure 'zeros' uses no non-locals (other than standard operators) and makes no assumptions other than a lower array bound of 1. A loop beginning

```
FOR i FROM LWB r TO UPB r . . .
```

makes no bound assumptions at all, and is therefore preferable for procedures which are to be kept for general use and intended to be fool-proof.

The generalization to arrays of more than one dimension should be obvious, and one example will suffice. This finds the coordinates of the highest mountain on a map represented as a two-dimensional array of reals.

```
PROC mountain  =  (REF[ , ]REAL map, REF INT x, y)VOID:
BEGIN
    REAL max  := 0.0;
    FOR i FROM 1 LWB map TO 1 UPB map
    DO FOR j FROM 2 LWB map TO 2 UPB map
       DO IF map[i, j] > max
          THEN max := map[i, j];   x := i;   y := j
          FI
       OD
    OD
END
```

A plain array mode, rather than a reference, should be used for the formal parameter if it is wished to protect the array against alteration by accidental assignment to the (formal) parameter. If the actual parameter is a variable, it will then be dereferenced before being identified with the formal parameter. In RS systems, this does not entail copying of the array elements, and therefore introduces no extra overheads, but it does leave open the possibility of the formal parameter getting altered as a result of non-local assignment to the *actual* parameter. If a copy of the array is required for use by the procedure, it can be created by declaring a local variable in the procedure and assigning the formal parameter to it.

A plain array mode must also be used if it is intended that a row display should be allowed as the actual parameter. For example, a procedure to sum the squares of the elements of a row of integers could be declared and used as follows.

```
PROC sumsq = ([ ]INT a)INT:
BEGIN
    INT sum := 0;
    FOR i TO UPB a
    DO sum PLUSAB a[i] ** 2 OD;
    sum
END;

INT n := sumsq((1, 2, 3, 4, 5)),
    m := sumsq(6)
```

The last step is shown as a reminder that the rowing coercion will convert 6 from INT to [ ]INT to satisfy the procedure.

It should be noticed that the square brackets in the mode of a formal parameter never contain bounds. The mode is, in effect, on the left-hand side of an identity declaration, where array size information is never given. The assignment to n in the above example is equivalent to

```
INT n := BEGIN [ ]INT a = (1, 2, 3, 4, 5);
               INT sum := 0;
               FOR i TO UPB a
               DO sum PLUSAB a[i] ** 2 OD;
               sum
         END
```

The fact that an array parameter can have any number of elements can be used to obtain the effect of a variable number of parameters. For example, a procedure to assign some constant to any number of real variables could be written and used as follows.

```
PROC multiassign = (REAL c, [ ]REF REAL vars)VOID:
                   FOR i TO UPB vars
                   DO vars[i] := c OD;
REAL u, v, w, x, y, z;
multiassign(pi, (u, v, w, x, y, z))
```

5.4.4 Procedure parameters

The phrase 'procedure parameter' is unfortunately ambiguous. In this section it is not intended to mean simply 'parameter of a procedure'. It means a parameter which is itself a procedure. Not a procedure call, but a procedure. This is a vital distinction to make at the outset. To write f(sqrt(x)) is to supply f with a REAL parameter. To write g(sqrt) is to supply g with a PROC(REAL)REAL parameter.

A procedure parameter enables a routine text to include calls of an unknown procedure. It is, of course, commonplace for a routine text to include calls of known procedures, which may have been declared locally or non-locally. To call an *unknown* procedure in a routine text means calling a procedure whose actual identity is not known when the text is written. If the need to do this should arise, it can be handled either by means of a non-local procedure *variable* (as discussed in Section 5.7) or by a procedure parameter.

To give these ideas definite shape, we shall take a very simple problem, more elaborate versions of which are a common occurrence in scientific work.

> Write a procedure which will sum any mathematical
> series to n terms, given a formula for the general term.

Such a procedure, given the formula 1/r and an integer n, should deliver as its result

$$1/1 \quad + \quad 1/2 \quad + \quad 1/3 \quad + \quad \ldots \quad \ldots \quad + \quad 1/n$$

or equally, given the formula r*r and an integer n, should deliver

$$1*1 \quad + \quad 2*2 \quad + \quad 3*3 \quad + \quad \ldots \quad \ldots \quad + \quad n*n$$

A formula like 1/r or r*r can be expressed as a PROC(INT)REAL, and the procedure which solves the problem takes this as a parameter:

```
PROC series = (PROC(INT)REAL formula, INT terms)REAL:
BEGIN
      REAL total := 0.0;
      FOR i TO terms DO total PLUSAB formula(i) OD;
      total
END
```

A program to sum the reciprocals of the first 1000 integers can therefore be written as

```
PROGRAM procparam
BEGIN
      PROC series = (PROC(INT)REAL f, INT n)REAL:
                    BEGIN REAL total := 0.0;
                             FOR i TO n
                             DO total PLUSAB f(i) OD;
                             total
                    END;
      PROC recip = (INT n)REAL: 1/n;
      write(("sum of reciprocals of integers to 1000 =",
            series(recip, 1000)))
END FINISH
```

In the call of a procedure like 'series', the procedure parameter can be given as an identifier like 'recip' or as any unit which will deliver the required procedure. One such unit is the routine text itself, for this *is* the procedure. The declaration of 'recip' could therefore be omitted, and the call of write be replaced by

    write(("sum of reciprocals of integers to 1000 =",
        series((INT n)REAL: 1/n, 1000)))

Supplying a formula is only one of numerous uses of procedure parameters. Another is to provide an escape route from a procedure to some label in the program. To illustrate this in a simple way, consider the following 'safe' square root procedure.

    PROC root = (REAL arg, PROC REAL bother)REAL:
    IF arg >= 0.0 THEN sqrt(arg) ELSE bother FI

This procedure could be called by

    root(x, GOTO remedy)

where 'remedy' is some label in the program accessible from this point. It would not matter whether the call of root was embedded in a formula or any other construction; on detecting a negative value of x, that context would simply be abandoned and the jump executed. Notice that the jump is used as the actual parameter in a strong context expecting a PROC REAL. There is no need to embody it in a routine text.

5.5 Procedures with no parameters

If a procedure requires no data, or can safely use non-locals as its source of data, it need not have parameters. The standard procedure 'random' is one example; this PROC REAL uses no program data, and when obeyed it delivers a REAL random number between 0 and 1. An example involving a parameterless procedure using non-local data is shown in Section 5.3.1.

The way in which a parameterless procedure is called gives rise to a notational ambiguity which must be resolved from the context. Usually, a procedure call is recognizable as such from the presence of the actual parameters. Thus sqrt(x) is a procedure call, whereas sqrt by itself is not. With a parameterless procedure, only the context makes it clear whether or not the procedure will be obeyed. For example, in the initialized variable declaration

    PROC REAL p := random

random is *not* obeyed. It is treated as an object of mode PROC REAL, as required for assignment to the procedure variable p. (Such variables are further discussed in Section 5.7.) However, in the declaration

    REAL x := random

the procedure random *is* obeyed in order that the right-hand side should produce the REAL result required for assignment to x. This can be looked upon as a coercion, as the context forces the PROC REAL to become a REAL. The coercion, which is called *deproceduring*, can take place in any type of context, including operand positions and even the left-hand sides of assignments. The latter is, however, rare—as the left-hand side would have to be a parameterless procedure delivering a reference as its result.

As explained in Chapter 2, any result from a program step followed by a semi-colon is simply discarded. This is the *voiding* coercion, applied in response to the strong VOID position occupied by an intermediate program step. (The body of a procedure occupies a similar position if the mode of the procedure specifies a VOID result.) An interesting question arises when the call of a parameterless procedure is used in such a context, as in the episode shown below. The procedure 'throw' is a PROC VOID which simulates the throw of a die, assigning a random integer to 'die' and delivering no result. When 'throw' is used as a step, it might not seem obvious whether it would be deprocedured, i.e. obeyed giving a VOID result, or simply discarded without being obeyed at all. It is in fact treated as a procedure call and obeyed, as the programmer obviously intends.

```
INT die;
PROC throw = VOID: die : = ROUND(0.5 + 6 * random);
. . .
throw;
```

Now consider the following continuation, in which throw is assigned to a procedure variable 'count'.

```
PROC VOID count;
count : = throw;
. . .
count;
```

In this last step, count is dereferenced and deprocedured. In other words throw is again obeyed. In the assignment step, throw is not obeyed on the right-hand side but is assigned straight away to count. However, count is then the result of the assignment and therefore of the step as a whole. Is it then to be dereferenced and deprocedured? It is not, for in a strong VOID context the result of an assignment is always voided at once.

5.6 Modes of result

The result delivered by a procedure to its context can have any mode, but those found most useful are the simple modes and VOID. Results of mode INT or REAL enable a procedure to be used in conjunction with the many standard operators which take INT or REAL operands. A result of mode BOOL is satisfyingly easy to use in a conditional.

Except for objects of mode STRING, arrays as results of procedures are used comparatively seldom. It is more usual to pass an array back to the program through a reference parameter, and there are good reasons for this practice. If the procedure delivers an actual array as its result, unnecessary overheads of copying are likely to be entailed. If on the other hand the procedure delivers an array reference, it must be valid outside the routine text. If the reference has been created by the routine, it has to be a HEAP variable for the reasons explained in Section 3.2.1, and this too carries overheads. This leaves the possibility of delivering a reference that is a non-local variable. But the best way for a procedure to use such a variable is to have it passed in as a parameter, in which case the parameter can serve as the output vehicle at the same time. It is, of course, possible to assign a result to a reference parameter and also deliver it. This is shown in the following procedure, which squares every element in a row of reals and delivers the array reference.

> PROC sq = (REF[ ]REAL v)REF[ ]REAL:
> (FOR i TO UPB v DO v[i] TIMESAB v[i] OD; v)

To understand this procedure properly, it is essential to distinguish between the range of an identifier and the lifetime of a reference. The identifier v, being a formal parameter of the routine text, has as its range the body of the routine, but the *actual* parameter will exist before, during and after the obeying of the procedure.

All of the above considerations apply equally to data structures in general. Large data structures in particular are usually best handled in terms of references.

The result delivered by a procedure can be a procedure, but the usefulness of this facility is somewhat limited as it is not possible to compute a new procedure in Algol 68. All that can be done, in effect, is to make a choice from a number of given procedures, taking care that the selected procedure will be a valid object outside the routine text which delivers it. The lifetime of a procedure is explained in the next section.

5.7 Procedures as objects

Objects in Algol 68 have modes, can be identified, used in expressions and assigned to variables. All of these characteristics are possessed by procedures. The mode of a procedure has been described in Section 5.2, and the abbreviated identity declaration in Section 5.3. The more general form of identity declaration, less often used, follows the standard pattern

> *mode identifier* = *unit*

A routine text is one form of unit, and only when the *unit* takes this form can the *mode* be abbreviated to PROC as in Section 5.3. When the *mode* is given in full, the *unit* can be anything which will deliver a procedure. For example,

> PROC(REAL)REAL wave = IF quad THEN sin ELSE cos FI

where 'quad' is some boolean, and sin and cos are the standard trigonometric functions of mode PROC(REAL)REAL.

A procedure variable is a reference to a procedure of some specified mode. For example, the declaration

> PROC(REAL)REAL p

declares p as a variable of mode REF PROC(REAL)REAL. Procedures such as sqrt can now be *assigned* to p, thus

> p := sqrt

and when p(x) is written, p is dereferenced and sqrt(x) is taken. Procedure variable declarations can, of course, be initialized, and if the right-hand side is a routine text, the mode of the procedure can be abbreviated to PROC on the left, as in identity declarations.

Procedure variables are needed in RS systems for the declaration of mutually recursive procedures. This is a specialized technique in which each of two procedures includes within its routine text a call of the other. (More generally, there may be a whole set of such procedures, but the principle is the same.) The difficulty is that, in RS systems at least, identifiers must be declared before they are used, and this makes it seem impossible to declare either of the procedures before the other. The difficulty is easily overcome by use of a procedure variable. For convenience, we shall use procedures of mode PROC(INT)INT in the following pattern, but any modes would do, and they need not be the same.

> PROC(INT)INT v;
>
> PROC p = (INT n)INT:
> > *unit including v in a procedure call* ;
>
> v := (INT n)INT:
> > *unit including a call of p*

It can be seen that no identifier has been used before it has been declared, and once the assignment has been made to v, any calls of p or of the procedure referred to by v can be obeyed.

Simple recursion in which a procedure calls itself can be expressed in the normal manner, for RS systems do permit a routine text to use the identifier given to it in an abbreviated procedure declaration. The usual example is

> PROC factorial = (INT n)INT:
> IF n = 0 THEN 1 ELSE n * factorial(n − 1) FI

Though having the merit of brevity, this example is not the most efficient way to compute a factorial. Recursive methods are best suited to non-numerical problems such as route finding, game playing and tree processing. Some examples of recursive methods in list processing will be found in Section 6.7.2, but generally if a non-recursive solution to a problem is easily written, it should be used instead.

The use of procedure variables makes it necessary to consider the lifetimes of procedures as objects. When a routine text is assigned to a procedure variable, it must not use any non-locals whose ranges are less than the range of the variable. The assignment in the following episode is wrong because the routine text assigned to w uses n, which has gone out of range by the time w is used.

```
PROC(INT)INT w;
BEGIN
    INT n;
    read(n);
    w := (INT i)INT: i + n      ???
END;
write (w(4))
```

In another form of this mistake, the assignment is made in the text of a routine rather than the simple closed clause shown here, and the non-local of the inner routine text is a formal parameter of the outer. The principle is exactly the same.

5.8 Operator declarations

A program can include declarations of new operators, and add to the meanings of existing standard operators. Monadic and dyadic operators are much like procedures taking one or two parameters respectively, with certain differences of syntax and semantics to be described in this section.

Syntactically, the activation of an operator is simpler than the call of a procedure, as is obvious from the comparison of + with a hypothetical 'plus' procedure:

    operation   *procedure call*

      x + y   plus (x, y)

A more fundamental difference, however, is that the same operator symbol can be defined to have different meanings for operands of different modes, and can have monadic definitions along with dyadic ones. All this variety is possible in the same range of the program by redeclaring the operator for each new meaning. Whenever the operator is used, the actual operand modes determine which definition will be selected, and this places certain constraints on the types of coercion for operands. The only coercions applied to operands are dereferencing, deproceduring and uniting (this last being described in Section 6.8). It follows that no two operator definitions in a given range may differ only in the number of REFs or PROCs on the modes of their operands.

An operator is declared like a procedure with one or two parameters, but with OP in place of PROC. The usual abbreviated form of declaration is thus

    OP *opsymbol* = *routine-text*

This is not an identity declaration, as an operator is not an 'object' and does not, in fact, have a mode. An *opsymbol* can be one of a selected list of symbols such as <, or a compound symbol such as < =, or a bold word such as PLUS. The detailed rules applying to RS systems are given in Appendix 1. An operator declaration can also take one of the more general forms

    OP (*mode*) *mode opsymbol* = *unit*

for a monadic definition, or

    OP (*mode , mode*) *mode opsymbol* = *unit*

for a dyadic definition. The unit must deliver an object of the corresponding PROC mode (for example a PROC(REAL)REAL for an OP(REAL)REAL type of declaration).

As an example of an operator declaration, the one shown below adds a new meaning to the exponentiation operator $**$. This is a standard dyadic operator which always takes an INT as its right operand, that is, it will raise its left operand to an integral power only. Such a definition avoids certain mathematical complexities, but there are occasions when fractional powers would be useful. For example, 2 to the power of one third could mean the real cube root of 2, as distinct from the two complex roots. To calculate such a fractional power, it is necessary to use logarithms, thus

   OP $**$ = (REAL x, y)REAL: exp(ln(x) $*$ y)

The definition gives rise to a fault if x is not positive. But there is another drawback. Although we can now write 2.0 $**$ (1/3), we still cannot write 2 $**$ (1/3). A further declaration is required for an INT left operand,

   OP $**$ = (INT x, REAL y)REAL: exp(ln(x) $*$ y)

The routine text happens to be the same in both cases, as x is widened from INT to REAL in the parameter of ln, but the separate operator definition was necessary as widening is not applied to operands. Since both of these operator declarations add extra meanings to an existing dyadic operator symbol, its existing priority of 8 applies.

When an entirely new operator symbol is being declared dyadically, or an existing one is being given its first dyadic meaning, the operator declaration may be preceded by a priority declaration of the form

   PRIO   *opsymbol*   =   *digit*

where the digit is in the range 1 to 9. This fixes the dyadic priority of *all* the dyadic meanings of that operator. There can be no more than one priority declaration for any given operator symbol in the same range. In the absence of a priority declaration or any existing priority, RS systems assume a priority of 1, which is the least binding.

To illustrate a set of declarations for a new operator symbol, we return to the matter of raising numbers to REAL powers. Instead of extending the standard operator, we could declare a new one, RTP ('raised to power'), thus

   PRIO RTP = 8;
   OP RTP = (INT x, y)INT: x $**$ y,
      RTP = (REAL x, INT y)REAL: x $**$ y,
      RTP = (REAL x, y)REAL: exp(ln(x) $*$ y),
      RTP = (INT x, REAL y)REAL: exp(ln(x) $*$ y)

Only the OP(REAL, INT)REAL meaning permits a negative left operand. The four definitions are presented here as one composite declaration using commas for separation. They could equally well have been written as separate declarations with semi-colons and with the word OP repeated.

It can be seen that defining new meanings for arithmetical operators or introducing new arithmetical operators may involve considerable effort. Even the four definitions above do not include LONG or COMPL modes of left operand, as does the standard exponentiation operator. Operator declarations are mainly useful as an adjunct to user-defined data structures, enabling these to be used in formulae and not just as parameters of procedures. Examples of such use will be found in Section 6.3 and towards the end of Section 6.8.1.

6 Data structuring

6.1 The purpose of data structuring

Items of data often possess more than one attribute. A meteorological observation may comprise separate measurements of air temperature, pressure, wind direction and velocity, to mention only a few. An ordinary pair of spectacles is optically defined by six or more REAL values. The medical condition of a patient could include values of mode STRING ('satisfactory'), REAL (blood pressure), INT (days ill) and BOOL (whether conscious). Grouping of values in a STRUCT mode enables all the techniques already described for values of simple modes to be extended and applied to these structured values. An object with a STRUCT mode can (where appropriate) be treated as a single entity for input, output, assignment, as an operand, parameter of a procedure, or result. For example, if 'data' is a structured value and x is a variable of corresponding mode, the assignment

$$x \quad := \quad data$$

copies the entire structure into x for later use. The fact that 'data' has several distinct components ('fields') can be forgotten until they are individually required. This will of course eventually occur, but the splitting of a structure into fields can often be confined within procedures and operators. This keeps the outer levels of a program free from superfluous detail.

One of the most interesting and important tasks in program planning—on which the success or failure of a large program may easily depend—is deciding on the form of data structuring which will best fit the problem. Usually a mixture of arrays and structures will be required, arrays for large sets of similar items and structures for groups of related values like those already mentioned. Very commonly, the key mode is an array of structures—a whole set of identically structured items.

The crucial distinction between an array and a structure is that an element of an array can be selected dynamically by a computed subscript, whilst a field of a structure can be selected only by its field selector, which cannot be computed. In consequence, the implementation overheads of structures are negligible.

In non-numerical work, one of the most useful applications of structures is 'list processing'. By including in a structure a reference to another structure, items of data can be chained together with great flexibility. Such chains may be linear or branching, and can be extended or contracted dynamically without any unaffected items having to be copied. For this type of computing, described in Section 6.7, structures are more powerful than arrays.

6.2 Structure modes

To suit the problem in hand, one is free to make up any desired structure mode with any number of fields of any mode, such as

STRUCT(INT qty, partno, STRING descrip)

An object of this mode would comprise two integers and a string. When fields of the same mode are adjacent, the mode need only be written for the first. The field selectors have the same form as identifiers, but they are not classed as such. *They are parts of the mode.* The above with 'quantity' instead of 'qty', or with the fields in a different order, would constitute a wholly different mode. In any one structure, the field selectors must obviously all be different, but selectors used in one mode can be used in other modes without giving rise to any ambiguity. Furthermore, a selector can be the same as an identifier in the same range of the program, for the two are always distinguishable from the contexts in which they are used.

It is often convenient to invent a new bold word as a shorter way of expressing a STRUCT mode, and declare this in a *mode declaration*, as in the following episode. New mode names can be declared for any types of mode, not only STRUCT modes, and further details are given in Section 6.4.

MODE PACK = STRUCT(INT qty, partno, STRING descrip);
PACK biggest = (1, 1000, "piano");
PACK mine : = biggest;
[20]PACK kit;
read(kit)

Structures do not have denotations, but they can be represented by collateral displays in strong positions, as shown in the identity declaration for the structure constant 'biggest'. The assignment of 'biggest' to 'mine' copies the whole PACK into the space created by this variable declaration. The array variable 'kit' has space for 20 structures of mode PACK, and as each has three fields the step 'read(kit)' inputs 60 items of data in all.

6.2.1 Field selection
To select a field from a structure, the 'selection' construction

selector OF *s*

is used. If *s* is a constant structure (mode STRUCT . . .), this gives the required field with the mode given in the structure mode. Thus

qty OF biggest

has mode INT. But if *s* is a structure variable (mode REF STRUCT . . .), the REF is transferred to the selected field. Thus

descrip OF mine

applies to the STRING field of a REF PACK and therefore has mode REF

STRING. This makes it possible to assign field values to structure variables individually, as for example

    descrip OF mine : = "grand piano";
    partno OF mine : = 1001

Field selection thus behaves in a similar way to array indexing, and the similarity extends to multiple references. If field selection is applied to a multiple REF, it causes dereferencing until a single REF remains (i.e. mode REF STRUCT . . .) and this remaining REF is then transferred to the selected field as before.

Field selection can also be applied to an array of structures or a reference to such. The '[ ]' or 'REF[ ]' is then transferred to the selected field. For example, in the previous section, the mode of 'kit' written out in full is

    REF[ ]STRUCT(INT qty, partno, STRING descrip)

and so

    qty OF kit

has mode REF[ ]INT, referring to the 20 integer fields of the structures held in 'kit'. The bounds are the same as for the array of structures, namely 1:20. The step 'read(qty OF kit)' would input the 20 integers.

6.2.2 Binding rules for selection

A selection is a close-knit entity which can be used as an operand in a formula without needing brackets. Thus, the first operand of PLUSAB in the formula

    partno OF mine PLUSAB 3

is 'partno OF mine'. This syntactic point is summarized in the first of the following rules for selections:

    Rule 1   'OF' binds more tightly than any operator
    Rule 2   Brackets bind more tightly than 'OF'

The purpose of the second rule is to settle the meanings of constructions like

    a OF p(x)
    a OF r[n]

In the first, p(x) is a procedure call and the selection applies to the result delivered by the procedure. In the second, r[n] is an array element and the selection is applied to it. If a *selection* is to be parameterized or indexed, brackets are needed round the selection, as in

    (p OF s)(x)
    (r OF s)[n]

which could represent the call of a procedure field and the indexing of an array field of a structure s. (Rows as fields of structures are further discussed in Section 6.5.)

After 'OF', the allowed forms are primaries or further selections. A selection of a selection is shown in the last of the following steps.

```
MODE WIND = STRUCT(REAL direction, velocity);
MODE OBS = STRUCT(WIND w, REAL temp, press);
OBS s := ((0.0, 15.0), 8.5, 748.0);
read(direction OF w OF s)
```

Notice the use of a nested collateral to display a nested structure.

6.3 A short program with structured data

The program given below shows in miniature the typical pattern for computing with structured data—mode declarations, procedure and operator declarations (here just one operator declaration), input of data, computation and output. This program calculates the number of intersections of a set of 8 circles whose position and sizes are read in.

```
PROGRAM intersections
BEGIN
    MODE POINT = STRUCT(REAL x, y);
    MODE CIRCLE = STRUCT(POINT centre, REAL radius);
    PRIO LAPS = 1   COMMENT optional in RS systems COMMENT;
    OP LAPS = (CIRCLE a, b)BOOL:
    BEGIN
        REAL cc = (x OF centre OF a − x OF centre OF b)**2
                    + (y OF centre OF a − y OF centre OF b)**2;
        cc < (radius OF a + radius OF b)**2 AND
        cc > (radius OF a − radius OF b)**2
    END;

    [8]CIRCLE spot; read(spot);
    INT crossings := 0;

    FOR i TO UPB spot
    DO FOR j TO i − 1
        DO
          IF spot[i] LAPS spot[j]
          THEN crossings PLUSAB 2
          FI
        OD
    OD;

    write(("Number of crossings = ", crossings))
END
FINISH
```

It is instructive to compare this with a more old-fashioned type of solution, as shown below, using no data structuring other than the declaration of arrays. The unstructured solution is, in fact, slightly shorter; it avoids the extra writing involved in mode declarations and field selection. But two important points must be borne in mind. In a larger program, the position is usually reversed, as the setting up is a smaller proportion of the whole, and once it has been done, the rest of the program is shortened. The other important consideration is that extra *text* does not necessarily mean a longer compiled program, for mode declarations and field selections cost virtually nothing. The prime criterion for data structuring should be intelligibility.

```
PROGRAM oldstyle
BEGIN
    PROC laps = (REAL x1, y1, r1, x2, y2, r2)BOOL:
    BEGIN
        REAL cc = (x1 − x2)**2 + (y1 − y2)**2;
        cc < (r1 + r2)**2 AND cc > (r1 − r2)**2
    END;

    [8]REAL x, y, r;
    FOR i TO 8 DO read((x[i], y[i], r[i])) OD;
    INT crossings := 0;

    FOR i TO 8
    DO FOR j TO i − 1
        DO
            IF laps(x[i], y[i], r[i], x[j], y[j], r[j])
            THEN crossings PLUSAB 2
            FI
        OD
    OD;

    write(("Number of crossings = ", crossings))
END
FINISH
```

Both versions of this program could be shortened by eliminating the operator or procedure declaration which calculates whether two given circles overlap. As the routine is called into play only once, it could be written openly in the conditional, but the examples would then fail to model larger programs where preliminary operator or procedure declarations are the general rule.

6.4 Mode declarations

Mode declarations for naming structure modes have been used already in this chapter. Any type of mode can be named in this way, provided that the new bold word is not an existing bold word of the language (such as CASE). If the new mode name stands for an array mode, the size or pair of bounds must be included in the mode declaration, as in

```
MODE CHROMSCALE = [12]REAL
```

This enables CHROMSCALE to be used in a variable declaration or a generator—where size information is necessary. In other contexts, where the giving of size normally causes a fault, the size from the mode declaration is simply ignored. Evaluation of any expressions given in a mode declaration does not take place until the mode name is used for space generation. In the episode

```
INT n;
MODE SNAP = STRUCT(REAL aperture, time);
MODE FILM = STRUCT(STRING type, INT speed, [n]SNAP frames);
n := 36;
FILM f
```

the final declaration makes space for a FILM whose 'frames' field contains 36 SNAP elements.

Flexible array modes can be named in mode declarations. For example, the mode name STRING is already defined in Algol 68 as

```
MODE STRING = FLEX[0]CHAR
```

It will be recalled that flexibility can only apply to references. Where normally it would be illegal to write FLEX explicitly, it is ignored if it arises from a named mode. Thus the declarations

```
STRING language := "ALGOL 68";
STRING heading = "LIST OF SUCCESSFUL CANDIDATES"
```

are interpreted as meaning

```
FLEX[0]CHAR language := "ALGOL 68";
[ ]CHAR heading = "LIST OF SUCCESSFUL CANDIDATES"
```

The size 0 changes to 8 when initialization of 'language' takes place.

Mode declarations can be recursive, subject to the modes being actually realizable. No object of the mode defined must demand an infinite amount of space, and no ambiguities of coercion must arise from the mode definitions. An example of the first error is seen in

```
MODE INFIN = STRUCT(INT item, INFIN more)      ???
```

The infinite space requirement is clear from the attempted assignment

```
INFIN testcase := (1, (2, (3, (4, . . .     ???
```

which does not terminate. By contrast, the mode declaration

```
MODE PAIR = STRUCT(INT head, REF PAIR next)
```

is acceptable. An object of mode PAIR demands space only for one integer and one reference. This mode is, in fact, the basis of list structuring (Section 6.7). Modes such as

```
MODE AUX = REF AUX      ???
MODE VAL = PROC VAL      ???
```

are unacceptable because they would lead to ambiguity in determining coercions.

Mutually recursive modes are permitted, and the requirement in RS systems that nothing be used before it has been declared is satisfied by a special construction which serves as an 'intention to declare'. It is shown in

MODE Y,
    X = *mode definition involving Y* ,
    Y = *mode definition involving X*

This is all one step, and would be followed by a semi-colon. Its parts are separated by commas. The first part is a mention of Y which is enough to allow its use in later definitions before the end of the step as a whole. By the end of the step, the various definitions must all be complete. The word MODE appears once only. Consecutive mode declarations can always be grouped in this way if desired, but here it is essential.

6.5 Arrays in data structures

Structuring of data to fit a particular problem may require an array or a structure, and either of these may contain other arrays or structures as component parts. Alternatively, they may just contain *references* to other arrays and structures. This section discusses the factors which influence the choice, with special attention to array components. The choice can be seen in its simplest terms by comparing the following two variables:

    [5][7]INT fivesevens;
    [5]REF[ ]INT fiverefs

The first of these variables can hold five rows which all have the same size. There is in fact little to choose between 'fivesevens' and a two-dimensional array variable

    [5, 7]INT fivebyseven

The method of indexing is slightly different (fivesevens[i][j], fivebyseven[i,j]), but both are essentially rectangular in shape. The variable 'fiverefs' is quite different. Its five elements are references to other arrays altogether, and these can *all have different sizes*. The price to be paid is small; space for the subsidiary arrays must be generated separately. Five separate array variables could be declared and assigned to 'fiverefs', though it is normally easier to generate the references dynamically. For example, to set up the triangle of integers

    0
    1 0
    2 1 0
    3 2 1 0
    4 3 2 1 0

the simplest method would be

```
FOR i TO 5
DO fiverefs[i] := LOC[i]INT;
    FOR j TO i DO fiverefs[i][j] := i − j OD
OD
```

The extra reference in the mode of 'fiverefs' does not normally get in the way. The mode of fiverefs[i] is REF REF[ ]INT, but the mode of fiverefs[i][j] is REF INT, which is the same as the mode of fivesevens[i][j].

Exactly the same considerations apply to rows of structures which contain arrays or array references. Direct array fields must have the same size through the whole row of structures, as shown in

```
INT n;
MODE SET = STRUCT(REAL price, [n]REAL capacity);
n := 12;
[50]SET range
```

Although the size n could be different for different *individual* objects of mode SET, it cannot vary from one element to another in a *row* of SETs. This limits the usefulness of direct array fields, for in practical situations arrays in rows of structures usually need to vary in size. Such fields must either be flexible arrays or array *references*. For data which is to be read in by the program, array references may be considered preferable. This can be illustrated by considering how to input the following data into one variable.

(*20 subjects*)	(*Vols*)	(*Pages per vol*)
MUSIC		
	3	250 254 274
HISTORY		
	6	852 336 520 375 400 208
ALGOL 68		
	1	148
. . .		

The subjects are given as strings on separate lines, as a string item of data for reading by a program is terminated by the end of a line. The input can be accomplished by

```
MODE BOX = STRUCT(STRING subject, REF[ ]INT pages);
[20]BOX lib;
INT vols;
FOR i TO UPB lib
DO read((subject OF lib[i], vols));
    read((pages OF lib[i] := LOC[vols]INT, newline))
OD
```

The mode of 'pages OF lib[i]' is REF REF[ ]INT, to which a locally generated REF[ ]INT is assigned. It is into this latter reference that the numbers of pages per volume are to be input. It may not be clear that this is what will happen—for the result of an assignment is its *left*-hand side. However, the 'read' procedure cannot use this double reference, and dereferences to a single REF as the problem requires. The generator in this episode is chosen as a LOC rather than a HEAP generator because there are no declarations in the loop. The 'locality' therefore extends to the outer level of the episode. Had 'vols' been declared inside the loop—as might have been thought more stylish—locally generated space would be released *each time round the loop*. A HEAP generator would then have been required.

The alternative solution using a flexible array field is

```
MODE BOX = STRUCT(STRING subject, FLEX[0]INT pages);
[20]BOX lib;
FOR i TO UPB lib
DO INT vols;
    read((subject OF lib[i], vols));
    [vols]INT pages;
    read((pages, newline));
    pages OF lib[i] : = pages
OD
```

By contrast with the previous solution, in which the numbers of pages are read directly into the space they are finally to occupy, here they are read into a temporary variable and *copied* into the REF FLEX[ ]INT 'pages OF lib[i]'. The necessity for this double handling stems from there being no way of resetting the size of a flexible array variable other than by assignment of a whole array at once. Strings are exceptional. Input to 'subject OF lib[i]' can be achieved directly, even though its mode is REF FLEX[ ]CHAR, as the end of a line terminates a string on input.

6.6 Computing with references

6.6.1 Reference to common data

One of the uses of a reference is to avoid duplication of data. To include the same item of data in two different structures, it can of course be repeated in each. Alternatively, a single master copy can be held and references used in place of the data itself wherever required. This may be advantageous for two reasons. The item of data may be large—so a single copy saves space. And if the data has to be updated, there is only one copy to deal with, as shown in the following piece of program about scales of pay.

```
REAL normal : = 100.0,
      special : = 130.0;
MODE EMPLOYEE = STRUCT(STRING name, REF REAL pay);
[4]EMPLOYEE staff : = (("Baker", normal),
                       ("Carter", normal),
                       ("Smith", special),
                       ("Jones", normal));
. . . . . . . . .
normal : = 130.0
```

The last assignment increases the pay of Baker, Carter and Jones to 130.0 in one step. If the pay of an EMPLOYEE had been a REAL rather than a REF REAL, they would have required individual updating.

6.6.2 Testing a reference

When computing with references rather than actual values, the need for a new test of equality is quickly felt. The word 'IS' tests whether two *references* are the same or different. The ordinary equals operator will not do this—as is well illustrated by the following tests carried out after the foregoing program extract.

test	*result*
pay OF staff[3] = normal	TRUE
pay OF staff[3] IS normal	FALSE

The first of these two tests is an ordinary boolean formula. The modes of the two operands are REF REF REAL for 'pay OF staff[3]' and REF REAL for 'normal'. The equals operator is defined for REAL operands (amongst others) and here dereferences both sides to REAL. As they both give 130.0 the result of the test is TRUE; Smith's special pay is indeed equal in value to the normal pay received by the other three. The second of the two tests dereferences only far enough to reach the same *reference* mode on both sides. The comparison is therefore made at the REF REAL level, and the result is FALSE because 'special' and 'normal' are different variables.

The word 'IS' (and its opposite 'ISNT') is not an operator. No operator declaration can be used to alter or add to its meaning. Syntactically, therefore, 'a IS b' does not count as a formula. It is in fact a type of unit called an *identity relation*, whose two sides can be any expressions which produce references. In simple terms, IS and ISNT (like the assignment symbol : =) bind less tightly than any operator. This means that an identity relation can never be used as an operand in a formula unless brackets are used, thus

   (a IS b) AND (c ISNT d)

The two sides of an identity relation must both be references, and must have exactly the same mode after the number of references has been equalized by minimal dereferencing. If the same reference mode cannot be reached, a fault occurs.

Alternative representations of IS and ISNT are the compound symbols : = : and :/= : respectively.

6.6.3 The null reference

The expression NIL is a unique null reference of greatest use in list structures (Section 6.7). NIL does not refer to any actual object, and cannot be made to do so. It cannot be dereferenced—or a fault will occur—but it can be tested for.

An example of a use of NIL, continuing again from the episode in Section 6.6.1 is

   pay OF staff[2] : = NIL

This is a formal and *detectable* way of ensuring that 'pay OF staff[2]' no longer refers to any actual pay variable. To test whether 'pay OF staff[2]' contains NIL, the following form of identity relation can be used:

   REF REAL(pay OF staff[2]) IS NIL

After the previous assignment, this gives the result TRUE. The cast used here defines the level of reference being tested. The identity relation

   pay OF staff[2] IS NIL

gives FALSE, because it tests 'pay OF staff[2]', which is the variable *holding* the NIL; it is not NIL itself. This slight awkwardness suggests an alternative approach to the handling of NIL, summarized in the following steps,

   REF REAL nilpay = NIL;
   pay OF staff[2] : = nilpay;
   . . . . . .
   IF pay OF staff[2] IS nilpay THEN . . . . . .

Although nilpay is actually NIL, the identity declaration gives it a definite mode, which forces the required dereferencing of the left-hand side of the identity relation. In all other respects, nilpay is the same as NIL; it cannot be dereferenced, and if any assignment to nilpay is attempted, a fault occurs. This technique for handling NIL is preferred by many programmers as being safer and more expressive, especially when null references of various modes are required in the same program, as is often the case.

6.7 List structures

The term 'list structure' describes a particular way of holding data in a chain of structures connected by references. Each structure contains one or more items of data and a reference to a further structure. The system is particularly suitable for work where new items of data can appear and old ones disappear in continually changing, unforeseeable ways. To accumulate lists of items dynamically, arrays are not suitable because they cannot be extended. (Even flexible arrays cannot act like concertinas.) Structures not containing references are even less dynamic, the number of fields being fixed when the program is written. In list structures, new items can be introduced at any positions without interfering with existing items, and old items can be deleted without leaving gaps.

   The basic idea underlying the maintenance of a list structure is to generate space for each new item as and when required, and not by declaring variables in advance. To take full advantage of the technique, the space is generated on the heap. This ensures that it is retained for as long as required and then relinquished, independently of the nested syntactic structure of the program. This dynamic use of data space does, of course, carry certain overheads which may vary slightly from one system to another. Also, the actual amount of space needed for a list structure includes an overhead for the references—one per item of data. This is comparatively small for large items of data.

   Work with list structures begins with a recursive mode declaration such as

   MODE PAIR = STRUCT(INT head, REF PAIR next)

   In practice, the mode must be chosen to suit the work. Here an item of data is taken to be an integer. Consideration must also be given to the type of linking required. The mode PAIR will enable us to set up simple unbranching chains. For tree structures, there would be two or more reference fields. (A binary tree is briefly considered in Section 6.7.2.) Modes should always be chosen with care, and this includes the actual choice of names. Other possible mode names for a PAIR would be NODE, CELL or LINK, all of which have been used by other writers. In the early days of list processing, the two fields were called head and tail. The selector 'next' for referring to the next structure is now more customary.

Before setting up an actual list of integers, we must consider how the list will be terminated. To fill the last REF PAIR field, NIL can be used. Better still, as explained in Section 6.6.3, a suitable identifier can be declared with mode REF PAIR,

REF PAIR endlist = NIL

A list of 1, 2, 3 can now be set up by means of the heap declaration

HEAP PAIR intlist
:= (1, HEAP PAIR := (2, HEAP PAIR := (3, endlist)))

Each of the nested collateral clauses is, of course, a structure display. It is important to remember that a PAIR has just *two* fields, an INT and a reference to another PAIR for which space must be generated. The nesting can obviously be carried to any required depth.

The mode REF PAIR should be thought of as the *basic* mode of a list, even though it starts with REF. This is the secret of list handling; once the mental leap has been made, list manipulations will be found reasonably straightforward. In what follows, the word *list* always implies the mode REF PAIR. Notice, in passing, that 'intlist' is a list (of 1, 2 and 3) and so also is 'endlist' (containing nothing at all).

If a list is a REF PAIR, a variable suitable for holding a list will have the mode REF REF PAIR. Such a variable is declared by

REF PAIR listvar := endlist

List variables usually need to be initialized to NIL, as here. To make listvar hold the list of three integers given earlier, the single assignment 'listvar : = intlist' would do. But starting from scratch, it would be built up in three successive assignments, as shown below. Remember that listvar has been initialized to endlist and that assignments are carried out from right to left.

listvar := HEAP PAIR := (3, listvar);
listvar := HEAP PAIR := (2, listvar);
listvar := HEAP PAIR := (1, listvar)

The implications for looping should be obvious. The only coercion in these assignments is dereferencing of listvar to REF PAIR in each of the structure displays.

Items in a list are not as accessible as elements of an array. The most easily reached is the one at the front, given by

head OF listvar

After the previous steps, this refers to 1. It is a REF INT, because field selection dereferences listvar to REF PAIR and transfers this remaining REF to the selected INT field (as described in Section 6.2.1). Thus 'head OF listvar' can be used on the left of an assignment to alter the first item in the list, e.g.

    head OF listvar : = 8;
    head OF listvar : = 1
    COMMENT which restores the status quo COMMENT

By the same reasoning, the mode of

    next OF listvar

is REF REF PAIR, for again field selection dereferences listvar to REF PAIR and transfers this remaining REF to the selected REF PAIR field. So 'next OF listvar' is a variable of the same mode as listvar itself. It holds the original list one place further down, that is, it holds the list of 2 and 3. The assignment

    listvar : = next OF listvar

dereferences 'next OF listvar' and assigns the list of 2 and 3 to listvar itself. Two more of the same assignments would move listvar down to the end of the original list and leave it holding NIL. Such assignments do not mutilate the original list, though they may make it inaccessible. There is no way of reversing the movement of listvar. If a list is not to be lost, it must either have its own identifier (like 'intlist' earlier) or be held in some other list variable which can stay holding it at its start.

We are now in a position to 'process' a list, that is, to perform some operation on each item of data in turn. Consider the problem of writing out the integers in a list held in a given list variable v. By using listvar as the working variable, the given list will remain securely held by v. Thus, starting ab initio (assuming only the original mode declaration and that of 'endlist'),

    REF PAIR v : = endlist;
    . . . . . . COMMENT here some more assignments to v COMMENT
    REF PAIR listvar : = v;
    WHILE listvar ISNT endlist
    DO write(head OF listvar);
        listvar : = next OF listvar
    OD

The termination condition for the loop should be self-explanatory. If such a condition were inadvertently omitted, a fault would occur when 'head OF listvar' attempted to select a field of NIL.

Variables like 'listvar' are useful for processing a list without altering its structure. Such processing can easily include changes to the values of any items of data, as long as their positions in the list are not altered. In the following loop, for instance, all the odd numbers in the list are increased by 1.

```
WHILE listvar ISNT endlist
DO IF ODD head OF listvar
    THEN head OF listvar PLUSAB 1
    FI;
    listvar : = next OF listvar
OD
```

Ordinary list variables of mode REF REF PAIR are less convenient for amending the actual structure of a list, such as deleting or inserting items. Consider, for instance, the problem of deleting any item in a list which is a zero. While moving listvar down the list, it is tempting to test 'head OF listvar' for 0. But when a zero has been found, it is too late to remove the item from the list. That would entail altering the reference field of the previous PAIR. To avoid this difficulty, one could look ahead and test 'head OF next OF listvar'—but the very first item in the list would then have to be treated as an exceptional case. To overcome these difficulties completely, a more powerful tool is needed.

6.7.1 The use of triple references

To alter the structure of a list, variables of mode REF REF REF PAIR are used. The technique is not immediately obvious, and is best explained in terms of a specific task. The task most commonly encountered is that of appending a new item at the far end of a list. It is, of course, much easier to add new items at the front of a list—as shown in the previous section where a list containing the first three integers was built up from pairs containing 3, 2 and 1 in that order. For practical purposes, lists so constructed are usually the wrong way round. The problem of adding to the far end of a list is therefore important.

Adding a new item at the end of a list involves replacing its final NIL, 'endlist', by a new REF PAIR such as

HEAP PAIR : = (n, endlist)

To see how this is done for a list of unknown length, we shall proceed by easy stages. The list to be amended is assumed to be held in an ordinary list variable, listvar (say). If the given list happened to be empty, listvar would hold endlist, and the required step would be

listvar : = HEAP PAIR : = (n, endlist)

If the given list contained just one item, 'next OF listvar' would hold endlist, and the required step would be

next OF listvar : = HEAP PAIR : = (n, endlist)

Similarly, for a list already containing two items, the step needed would be

next OF next OF listvar : = HEAP PAIR : = (n, endlist)

Each of these left-hand sides has mode REF REF PAIR and refers to endlist. When we do not know how many items there are in the given list, each REF REF

PAIR must be taken in turn and tested to see if it holds endlist. When endlist is found, the assignment can be carried out. To try one REF REF PAIR after another involves the use of a variable which can hold a REF REF PAIR, and such a variable has the mode REF REF REF PAIR. Initially it is made to hold listvar, thus

    REF REF PAIR p : = listvar;

The loop to find endlist is

    WHILE p ISNT endlist DO p : = next OF p OD;

   In the test for endlist, p is as good as listvar, next OF listvar, etc., as it is simply dereferenced twice instead of once. The same applies to the use of p in 'next OF p'. On completion of the loop, the variable held in p will be the one holding the empty list, endlist. The triple reference has now served its purpose, for the assignment must be made to the REF REF PAIR, which necessitates a cast.

    REF REF PAIR(p) : = HEAP PAIR : = (4, endlist)

Expressed in the form of a procedure, the method can be summarized as follows.

    PROC append = (REF REF PAIR v, INT n)VOID:
    BEGIN
        REF REF PAIR p : = v;
        WHILE p ISNT endlist DO p : = next OF p OD;
        REF REF PAIR(p) : = HEAP PAIR : = (n, endlist)
    END

Notice that the generators used for list processing *must* be HEAP generators if procedures such as this are to be used.

   The triple reference technique lends itself to any problems of list amendment, such as inserting or deleting items at any positions in a list. Its special merit is its ability to deal with lists of any length including zero length. However, amendments which do not alter the *structure* of the list can be handled in terms of ordinary list variables of mode REF REF PAIR.

6.7.2 Recursive methods

There has always been a close tie between list structures and the use of recursive procedures, as the recursive approach seems most natural for handling objects whose modes are themselves recursive. A recursive procedure is one whose body includes a call of itself. In processing a list, such a procedure starts by dealing with the first item of the list, and then calls itself to deal with the remainder. This is very well instanced in the recursive method of copying a list given later in this section.

   Attractive though the recursive method can be, it is not always the best way of solving a given problem because it can be extravagant in its use of workspace. Whenever a procedure is called, it has to remember the current state in readiness for its resumption, and this happens repeatedly. At some stage we may be in a procedure called in a procedure called in a procedure . . . ten or a hundred deep. Every one of these calls has a current position to remember. For a simple chain list of mode REF PAIR, the depth of recursion may be equal to the number of items in the list, and the method may therefore not be sensible or practical for long lists. Recursion really comes into its own for processing branching list structures (trees), because the depth of recursion is then much smaller than the number of items of data.

Three problems are considered in this section, two concerned with simple unbranching lists, and the third with a tree structure. In the first two problems, non-recursive and recursive solutions are compared. In the third problem, a non-recursive solution is hardly worth contemplating.

Problem 1

To make a new copy of a given list of mode REF PAIR, where

```
MODE PAIR = STRUCT(INT head, REF PAIR next);
REF PAIR endlist = NIL
```

The solution is to be given as a procedure with the given list as a REF PAIR parameter and its copy as the REF PAIR result.

The following is *not* a solution to the problem!

```
PROC cpy = (REF PAIR list)REF PAIR: HEAP PAIR := list
```

This copies the PAIR to which 'list' refers, but its 'next' field continues to refer to the original continuation. Furthermore, if 'list' happens to be endlist, the procedure faults by attempting to dereference NIL on the righthand side of the assignment. To make a new copy of a complete list structure, a new PAIR must be generated for *every* PAIR in the original list. The following is probably as good a non-recursive solution as any.

```
PROC copylist = (REF PAIR list)REF PAIR:
BEGIN REF PAIR listvar := list, copyvar;
       REF REF PAIR p := copyvar;
       WHILE listvar ISNT endlist
       DO REF REF PAIR(p) := HEAP PAIR;
          head OF p := head OF listvar;
          p := next OF p;
          listvar := next OF listvar
       OD;
       REF REF PAIR(p) := endlist;
       copyvar
END
```

By contrast, the recursive solution is easy to write, and shows more clearly what is happening:

```
PROC copylist = (REF PAIR list)REF PAIR:
IF list IS endlist THEN endlist
ELSE HEAP PAIR := (head OF list, copylist(next OF list))
FI
```

It is most important to test for the end of the list at the very outset, as shown here.

Problem 2

To find the number associated with a given string in a list of mode REF WORDS, where

```
MODE WORDS  =  STRUCT(STRING word, INT number, REF WORDS
                    next);
REF WORDS nil  =  NIL
```

If the given string is not in the list, the answer required is zero.

Whilst the non-recursive solution to this problem is quite simple, it holds one or two traps for the unwary programmer.

```
PROC stringval  =  (STRING s, REF WORDS list)INT:
BEGIN
    REF WORDS listvar  : =  list;
    WHILE (listvar ISNT nil) ANDTH word OF listvar / = s
    DO listvar  : =  next OF listvar OD;
    IF listvar IS nil THEN 0 ELSE number OF listvar FI
END
```

The operator ANDTH used in the WHILE part of the loop can be read as 'and then'. This is one of two special optimized boolean operators provided in RS systems in addition to the ordinary ones. In standard Algol 68, all dyadic operators—including AND and OR—evaluate both of their operands under all circumstances. The RS operator ANDTH (and its sister OREL) evaluates the left operand first, and then, but only if necessary, the right operand. Thus if the left operand of ANDTH is FALSE, the right operand is not evaluated, because the final result must be FALSE. (Similarly, if the left operand of OREL is TRUE, the right operand is not evaluated, because the result must be TRUE.) In the above procedure, the use of ANDTH is convenient, for when listvar holds NIL, no attempt is made to evaluate 'word OF listvar'. Such an attempt would cause a fault, as field selection cannot be carried out on a null reference. In passing, notice the brackets round the identity relation 'listvar ISNT nil'. These brackets are easily forgotten. They are necessary to convert the identity relation into a primary for use as an operand. (IS and ISNT bind less tightly than any operators.)

To adhere strictly to standard Algol 68, the use of ANDTH must be avoided. If this seems desirable, the WHILE part of the loop in the above procedure should be replaced by

```
    WHILE IF listvar IS nil THEN FALSE ELSE word OF listvar / = s FI
```

Turning now to the recursive method, we find again the merit of simplicity:

```
PROC stringval  =  (STRING s, REF WORDS list)INT:
IF list IS nil THEN 0
ELIF word OF list  =  s
THEN number OF list
ELSE stringval(s, next OF list)
FI
```

As with problem 1, the depth of recursion may be as great as the number of items in the list, so that for very long lists the method might be unacceptable.

Problem 3

To find whether a given string is present in a tree structure of mode REF DICT, where

MODE DICT = STRUCT(STRING word, REF DICT left, right);
REF DICT niltree = NIL

The strings in a REF DICT are assumed to be ordered so that all those which can be reached down a left branch are 'less than' (that is, alphabetically precede) those which can be reached down the corresponding right branch.

Unlike the structures so far considered, which have only one item at each depth of reference, a REF DICT has potentially one item at the first depth, two at the second, four at the third and so on. There may, however, be missing branches, as any of the REF DICT fields may be 'niltree'. Tree structures such as this are important because the access route to any given item is short, which makes updating much more rapid than for a simple unbranching list. The recursive solution is

```
PROC present = (STRING word, REF DICT tree)BOOL:
IF tree IS niltree THEN FALSE
ELIF word < word OF tree THEN present(word, left OF tree)
ELIF word > word OF tree THEN present(word, right OF tree)
ELSE TRUE
FI
```

None of the problems discussed in this section has involved alteration to the *structure* of a list or tree, but no difficulty should be encountered in writing such procedures recursively. A suggested exercise for the reader is to write a procedure of mode

PROC(STRING, REF REF DICT)BOOL

to extend a given tree to include a given string, but do nothing if the string is found to be already present. The boolean result should indicate whether a new entry was actually made.

6.8 Unions

The data structuring arrangements so far described can bring together any number of individual values as component parts of one object. In particular, the STRUCT modes are convenient for describing the co-existing attributes of an object. They are less suitable for describing attributes which are mutually exclusive. This is where UNION modes may prove useful. Consider, for example, a program dealing with garments and their sizes, some types of garment being sized by integers and others by strings such as 'medium'. The mode UNION(INT, STRING) could handle sizes of either kind. A union mode can include any number of constituent modes, and these can be of any type, provided that no one is coercible to another by dereferencing or deproceduring. As with STRUCT modes, it is often convenient to declare a mode name for a union mode, such as

MODE SIZE = UNION(INT, STRING)

Although an object of mode SIZE will have originated from an INT or a STRING, it cannot be handled as an INT or as a STRING. The whole purpose of the union mode is to conceal this difference. As a united object, a SIZE can be passed to a procedure, used as an array element or as an item in a chain list, without regard to its original mode.

The uniting of a particular object into a given union mode is a form of coercion which takes place in strong contexts and in operand positions. An example of a strong context is the right-hand side of an assignment, as in the initialized variable declaration

SIZE s : = "medium"

The string 'medium' is in a strong UNION(INT, STRING) context and is coerced to that mode for assignment. The same variable could later undergo the assignment

s : = 32

where 32 is in the same strong context and is united to UNION(INT, STRING). Any object can be united, provided that its mode is a constituent of the union. An object which has already been united can be united to a larger union provided that *all* the constituent modes of the original union are present in the larger union, as is the case in

UNION(STRING, REAL, INT)t : = s

where s is the REF UNION(INT, STRING) already defined. The right-hand side in this example is first dereferenced and then united.

A union within a union is treated simply as the set of its constituents. Thus, in the mode

UNION(REAL, SIZE)

the mode SIZE loses its identity, simply contributing INT and STRING to make UNION(REAL, INT, STRING).

In addition to the ordinary modes, a union may also include the mode VOID, as in the variable declaration

UNION(REAL, INT, VOID)u : = EMPTY

The word EMPTY is the denotation for VOID (used only for this particular purpose). The assignment 'clears' the union variable, so that it holds no object at all.

6.8.1 The conformity clause

At some stage, it becomes necessary to convert an object with a union mode back to its original mode. There is no de-uniting coercion, but the program does retain knowledge of the current constituent mode of every united object. The only way in which this can be revealed, and the original object recaptured, is by means of a conformity clause. This type of clause resembles a CASE clause, in which the cases are selected according to the current constituent mode of a given united object. The form of the clause is shown below; the rules about ranges of identifiers are the same as those which apply to ordinary CASE clauses, given at the end of Section 3.4.2.

```
CASE  series delivering the united object
        IN ( mode optional-identifier ):   unit ,
            ( mode optional-identifier ):   unit ,
                 . . . . . .
        OUT  series
ESAC
```

Each 'case' after IN starts with a test mode, which must be a constituent of the given union (though it could be a sub-union). When a test mode is found which matches the mode from which the given object was originally united, the identifier—if given—identifies the de-united object. (If the test mode is a union itself, a match is found when the current mode of the object is included in the test mode.) The range of each optional identifier is the unit following, which is of course obeyed. Typically, this unit might consist of an assignment to a program variable of the appropriate mode. The test mode can be VOID if that mode is present in the given union. No identifier is required after VOID, and none must be given.

If no match of mode is found between IN and OUT, the series after OUT is obeyed. The OUT part of a conformity clause is optional but in RS systems a fault occurs if it is absent when it would have been selected. The conformity clause as a whole can deliver a result, and the usual balancing coercions are if necessary applied.

The purpose of structures and unions being to enable objects to be handled in general ways before descending to detail, it is a good plan to confine their decomposition to clearly defined sections of the program, preferably within routine texts. For example, a monadic operator for a SIZE operand could be

```
OP SMALL = (SIZE z)BOOL:
CASE z IN (INT n):  n < 34,
          (STRING s):  s = "SMALL"
ESAC
```

Such an operator could be applied to a united object of mode SIZE or even—since uniting takes place in operand contexts—to an object of mode INT or STRING. A further operator declaration such as

```
OP SMALL = (STRING s)BOOL: s = "S"
```

would not be allowed to co-exist with the previous declaration, as it would give rise to ambiguity. The rule is that co-existing operator definitions must never be applicable to the same modes of operand (or modes differing only in preliminary REFs and PROCs), whether in unions or not.

6.8.2 Unions and structures

This section introduces no new principles, but uses program extracts to show how data structuring may involve both STRUCT and UNION modes, the former for dealing with simultaneous attributes and the latter for mutually exclusive ones. The program is concerned with the management of a drinks cellar, and begins with the following declarations.

```
MODE WINE = STRUCT(REAL cost, INT year, STRING appellation),
      SCOTCH = STRUCT(REAL cost, BOOL blended),
      COGNAC = STRUCT(REAL cost, BYTES class);
MODE SPIRIT = UNION(SCOTCH, COGNAC),
      LIQUOR = UNION(WINE, SPIRIT, VOID);
MODE CELLAR = STRUCT(LIQUOR bottle, REF CELLAR next);
REF CELLAR endcellar = NIL
```

To appreciate this scheme, it is best to read upwards; the order given is a necessary consequence of declaration before use. A cellar is represented as a list of bottles of mode LIQUOR, each of which may be a WINE, SPIRIT or VOID.

Without some decomposition of the LIQUOR union, little meaningful processing of a list of bottles is possible (though EMPTY could be assigned to every bottle present). The program would therefore be likely to include procedures or operators for the testing of bottles, such as

```
OP VIN = (LIQUOR x)BOOL: (x ! (WINE): TRUE ! FALSE)
```

Notice that the contracted notation for CASE clauses (end of Section 3.4.2) is also allowed for conformity clauses. This operator answers the question 'is it true that this LIQUOR is WINE?'

Further examples of conformity clauses are shown in the following procedures, which process the whole of a given cellar. The first takes stock of the cellar and delivers the total cost of the bottles present. The second counts the empties.

```
PROC stockvalue = (REF CELLAR r)REAL:
BEGIN
    REF CELLAR cellarvar : = r;
    REAL value : = 0.0;
    WHILE cellarvar ISNT endcellar
    DO value PLUSAB CASE bottle OF cellarvar
                IN (WINE w): cost OF w,
                   (SCOTCH s): cost OF s,
                   (COGNAC c): cost OF c,
                   (VOID): 0.0
                ESAC;
        cellarvar : = next OF cellarvar
    OD;
    value
END;
```

```
PROC empties = (REF CELLAR r)INT:
BEGIN
    REF CELLAR cellarvar := r;
    INT emptyno := 0;
    WHILE cellarvar ISNT endcellar
    DO emptyno PLUSAB (bottle OF cellarvar ! (VOID): 1 ! 0);
        cellarvar := next OF cellarvar
    OD;
    emptyno
END
```

6.8.3 Ordering of constituent modes in RS systems

In RS systems, UNION(INT, REAL) is treated as though it were a different mode from UNION(REAL, INT). The order of the constituent modes is taken into account whenever two union modes have to be matched.

As a simple illustration, consider

```
MODE USI = UNION(STRING, INT),
     UIS = UNION(INT, STRING);
USI u := "xyz";
REF UIS r := u      ???
```

In the final step, no uniting has been called for; a match is sought between the modes REF UNION(INT, STRING) and REF UNION(STRING, INT). The equivalence of these modes passes unrecognized in RS systems, and a mode fault occurs. However, a step such as

```
UIS t := u
```

does prove to be acceptable, as the REF USI on the right-hand side can be dereferenced and then united to UIS before the assignment is carried out. This is possible because each of the constituents of USI is present in UIS, so the condition for uniting is satisfied.

If a union mode is written as a union containing other unions, repetitions of constituents are likely to occur, as in

```
UNION(INT, REAL, UIS)
```

This mode is equivalent to UNION(INT, REAL, STRING), the order of the constituents being defined as the order of their first occurrences.

7 Transput

7.1 Terminology

'Transput' is a word usefully coined by the originators of Algol 68 to embrace both input and output and to supersede the abbreviation I/O. The procedures 'read' and 'write' which have been used without comment in the preceding chapters are concerned with *character transput*, the data and results being expressed externally in terms of characters and in forms which are intended to be humanly intelligible. When results are output solely for storage and subsequent input to a program, *binary transput* is normally used. As this largely eliminates the conversions between internal and external data representations, it is much faster. Algol 68 has more to say about character than binary transput; its structure is more intricate, and it is an essential part of almost every program.

Character transput can take place with or without the aid of *formats*. A format describes—in a language of its own—how characters are laid out on the pages of data or results. When used for input, formatting causes a fault to occur if the layout of the data presented to the program fails to conform exactly to the format laid down; input without formatting is, in the ordinary way, more practical. For output, on the other hand, formatting is both powerful and useful, enabling quite complicated layout designs to be achieved with little effort. For many types of data structure, layout can be inserted between elements and fields without explicit decomposition in the program.

A program is allowed to use any number of transput *channels* having properties which reflect the attributes of different types of physical device. For example, a channel for use with a disc would allow random access for binary input and output, whilst a typical channel for a line printer would allow only sequential output of characters, line by line. For greatest simplicity in normal use, Algol 68 makes available three standard channels as a matter of course, one for character input, one for character output and one for binary transput. On these channels, the procedures used are:

type of transput	input	output
character	read	write or print
formatted character	readf	writef or printf
binary	readbin	writebin

The identifiers 'write' and 'print' are precisely equivalent, as also are 'writef' and 'printf'. The procedures 'read' and 'readf' both use the same standard character input channel, and similarly 'write' and 'writef' use the same standard output channel. By interspersing calls of 'read' and 'readf', or 'write' and 'writef', part of the transput on one channel can be conducted with formats and part without. All the above procedures take just one parameter, and this we shall call the *transput parameter*.

Somehow a program must keep track of the happenings on each channel currently in use. For example, it may need to know the position which has been reached in the external data. Position is described in terms of a character number within the current line (even for binary transput), a line number within the current page, and a page number within the notional *book* to which the channel is attached. The word 'book' must be understood as some source or sink of data, such as a filestore file in a large computer system. The three position integers are all set to 1 before transput begins, and their running values are held, along with other control information, in what is called a *file variable* of mode REF FILE. For the standard channels, file variables are already provided and initialized before the beginning of the user's program. They are 'standin' used by read and readf, 'standout' used by write and writef, and 'standback' used by readbin and writebin. Knowledge of these variables is important when using certain library transput control procedures described in later sections of this chapter.

7.2 The transput parameter

The parameter of a transput procedure can be a single item or a bracketed sequence of any number of assorted items. For example, the four calls

read(x);   read(p);   read(q);   read(v)

can be condensed into the single call

read((x, p, q, v))

The extra parentheses are necessary to make the four items into a single parameter (x, p, q, v). To put

read (x, p, q, v)   ???

is wrong because it gives four parameters instead of one.

All items in the transput parameter can be expressed in the form of units. For output, these must yield actual values. For input, they must yield references—that is, destinations for the values being read in. The values themselves can have any of the basic modes listed in Appendix 2, but cannot be references, unions, routines or formats. Groups of values can be transput together, to or from arrays and structures in the program—again with the proviso that no element or field has a REF, UNION, PROC or FORMAT mode. Elements of arrays are taken in ascending order of subscripting. Thus

[4]REAL a; read(a)

inputs a[1], a[2], a[3] and a[4]. For arrays of more than one dimension, the order is lexicographic in the subscripts, e.g.

[1, 1], [1, 2], ... [2, 1], [2, 2], ...

Fields of structures are taken in order from left to right.

Typical transput parameters are shown in the following piece of program.

```
MODE POINT = STRUCT(CHAR letter, REAL x, y);
POINT p, q;
read((p, newline, q, newline));
write(("THE DISTANCE BETWEEN ",
      letter OF p,
      " AND ",
      letter of q,
      " IS ",
      newline,
      sqrt((x OF p − x OF q)**2 + (y OF p − y OF q)**2),
      newline))
```

Positioning is achieved in this example by the use of 'newline' as an item in the transput parameter. This causes transput to continue from the start of the next line. Some data suitable for this episode could be

```
K    0      1.685     (DATUM)
J    253.8693   −0.5576   (FLAG POLE)
```

Rules for the spacing allowed between values, and the forms required for values of the various different modes, are given in Section 7.3. In the present example, after reading the letter and x and y fields of p, the effect of 'newline' is to skip past the comment (DATUM) and set the reading position ready for the same fields of q. The output produced by the above piece of program could be

```
THE DISTANCE BETWEEN K AND J IS
+2.5387920501145e +2
```

where e stands for 'times ten to the power of'. In default of any special action, the REAL value is given to the full length justified by its internal representation at the particular installation, and is expressed in the standard form with a tens exponent. This style of representation is usually called 'floating point'.

When the various units in a transput parameter are evaluated, their results may have to be coerced to modes suitable for the transput procedure. The only coercions which may be needed are, in fact dereferencing and deproceduring. For output, all initial REFs are removed, and for input all but one. By the normal coercion rules, this applies only to *whole items* in the transput parameter, not to the individual fields or elements of which they may be composed. Fields or elements which are references therefore have to be transput individually. Consider, for example, reading into

```
STRUCT(INT n, REF REAL f)s
```

This structure variable requires an INT and a REF REAL. Transput procedures cannot create references, and the fields must be taken separately, as in

```
read((n OF s, f OF s := LOC REAL))
```

The second item—the f OF s delivered by the assignment—has mode REF REF

REAL, and is dereferenced to REF REAL ready for input of a REAL value to the generated space. For output, the structure must be similarly decomposed. Thus

write((n OF s, f OF s))

causes the first item to be dereferenced once to reach an INT and the second twice to reach a REAL.

7.3 Representation of data

This section describes the forms of data acceptable for input by the procedure 'read' and produced as output by 'write' or 'print' (which, as already pointed out, are the same procedure).

7.3.1 Numbers

For input of a number, 'read' passes over spaces, new lines and new pages until a non-space character is reached. This is read as the first character of the number; reading then continues until the number is terminated by the end of the line or by any character which could not be a legal continuation, such as a space following a digit. The reading position is then left at the end of the line or at the terminating character, which is taken to be part of the next item. The value presented for input to a REAL variable need not contain a decimal point nor an exponent symbol—though if either is present it must come immediately after a digit in order that the number should not be terminated. The acceptable forms for integer, real and complex values are shown below. The characters used for the exponent and imaginary signs (e and i) may be subject to local variations. For instance, an upper case E may be permitted as an alternative to lower case e.

input integer value	*examples of input integers*
optional sign (and spaces)	`1234567`
digit(s)	`+    0`
input real value	*examples of input reals*
optional sign (and spaces)	`12.34567e-1`
digits optionally including point	`-1.2e+     6`
optionally,	`12345`
exponent symbol (and spaces)	`+.05`
optional sign (and spaces)	`+2658e-7`
digit(s)	`-   50e    10`
input complex value	*examples of input complex*
real value as above	`1   i   1`
optional spaces	`+3.0i-2.0`
imaginary symbol	
optional spaces	
real value	

For output of a number by 'write' or 'print', if there is not enough room left on the current line for the whole of the value, a new line—and if necessary a new page—is taken first automatically. The number of figures printed is installation dependent, and will also depend on the presence of SHORT or LONG in the mode (see Appendix 2). The standard output forms given below are accompanied by examples which reproduce the values given above for input. Arbitrary assumptions have been made about the number of figures in an integer ('int width'), a real '(real width') and an exponent ('exp width'). These and other width identifiers are, in fact, constants of mode INT set to appropriate values in each Algol 68 implementation. Further details will be found in Appendix 4.

output integer value
  [no of chars = int width + 2, but
  one less at start of a line]

  single space (omitted at start of line)
  spaces for any suppressed leading zeros
  sign
  digit(s)

examples of output integers
  [taking int width = 7]

  +1234567
        +0

output real value
  [no of chars = real width + exp width + 5,
  less 1 at the start of a line]

  single space (omitted at start of line)
  sign of mantissa
  first digit of mantissa
  point
  remaining digits of mantissa
  exponent symbol
  space for any suppressed zero in exponent
  sign of exponent
  digit(s) of exponent

examples of output reals
  [taking real width = 7
  and exp width = 2]

  +1.234567e +0
  -1.200000e +6
  +1.234500e +4
  +5.000000e -2
  +2.658000e -4
  -5.000000e+11

output complex value
  [no of chars = 2*(real width + exp width)
  + 11, less 1 at the start of a line]

  real value as before
  space
  imaginary symbol
  real value without initial space

examples of output complex
  [taking real width = 7
  and exp width = 2]

  +1.000000e +0 i+1.000000e +0
  +3,000000e +0 i-2.000000e +0

7.3.2 Characters and strings

This section describes the transput of characters and sequences of characters. A single character has mode CHAR, and a sequence may have mode [ ]CHAR, which is the same mode as STRING, or it may have one of the more primitive RS modes STRUCT *n* CHAR, where *n* is the number of characters in the sequence. In RS systems, the mode BYTES is defined as a particular character structure (see Section 4.4.1). For transput purposes, character structures behave just like fixed length rows of characters.

The character set which can be used in data streams is implementation dependent. Sequences of characters are not enclosed in quotes as they are in a program, and the quote character (″) is therefore treated like any other. No character has as its meaning 'take new line'—or, for that matter, a new page. However, the character set will always be found to include a *space character*. In a program, this can be denoted as a space in quotes (″ ″), or if preferred by means of the identifier 'blank', which is a standard constant of mode CHAR.

Input

For input to a CHAR variable, the very next character is read, even if it is a space character. If the reading position is at the end of a line, a new line—and page if necessary—is taken automatically first. For input to a [ ]CHAR variable, enough characters are read to fill the array, new lines and pages being taken automatically as necessary. However, for input to a STRING variable (REF FLEX[ ]CHAR), new lines are *not* taken. The end of the line terminates the string, and the upper bound of the STRING is set to the number of characters which were read. If the reading position is at the end of the line to start with, the string is taken as having no characters, and its upper bound is set to 0.

In addition to end of line termination of a STRING, any one of a given row of characters can be made to act as a string terminator. The row of characters is given as the second parameter in a call of the procedure 'make term'. For example

        make term (standin, ″0123456789″)

would cause any digit to terminate a STRING on the standard input channel until further notice. The terminating character is of course inspected, but is not actually *read*. It is not included in the string, but held over to be read as the first character in the next item of data.

Output

Output of characters and character strings is straightforward. Writing starts at the current writing position, and new lines and pages are taken automatically whenever required.

Example

We are given a data stream of the following type.

        12 plates, 6 knives, 6 ″sporks″, 1 cake stand.

Each item between the punctuation marks is to be read into a STRUCT(INT no, STRING things) variable, and printed out before the next item is read in. Output is required in the form

        +12 plates
         +6 knives
         +6 ″sporks″
         +1 cake stand

The number of items in the list is to be assumed unknown.

A solution (which presupposes that the list is not entirely empty) is

```
STRUCT(INT no, STRING things)s;
maketerm(standin, ",.");
CHAR c := ",";
WHILE c = "," DO read((s, c)); write((s, newline)) OD
```

Notice that 'things OF s' includes an initial space each time.

7.3.3 Booleans and BITS

The two boolean values denoted in a program by TRUE and FALSE are expressed in a data stream as single characters, usually T and F (but given at any installation by the CHAR constants 'flip' and 'flop'). Here we use T and F.

On input, spaces are passed over, and new lines and pages taken, when 'read' is searching for a BOOL. The first non-space character must be T or F, which puts TRUE or FALSE into the boolean variable. For output, the single character is printed, a new line or page being taken first if the printing position is at the end of a line.

For work with machine words, there is a mode BITS which, in formatless transput, behaves like a row of booleans. The actual number of bits in a BITS value is implementation dependent, and is given by the integer constant 'bits width', which we shall take here as 32 for ease of explanation. On input to a BITS variable, 'read' passes over spaces and takes new lines and pages as necessary until 32 T or F characters have been read. (No characters other than spaces must intervene.) On output, 32 characters T or F are printed, starting at the current writing position and taking a new line or page where necessary. It is often preferable for BITS values to be transput as sequences of digits in the scales of 2, 4, 8 or 16, for which formatted transput must be used (7.5.3.3).

7.4 Layout control

This section describes the standard procedures for ascertaining and altering the current reading or writing positions in character transput, and also includes a section on how to modify the styling of numbers when using 'write' or 'print'.

7.4.1 Relative positioning

Many examples already given have included 'newline' in the transput parameter. This is, in fact, a procedure itself and has the mode PROC(REF FILE)VOID. When given in the transput parameter, it causes 'read' to perform newline(standin) and 'write' to perform newline(standout). For example,

```
read((x, newline, y))
```

is entirely equivalent to

```
read(x); newline(standin); read(y)
```

The effect of newline is to make transput skip ahead to the start of the next line. There are four such repositioning procedures, all of mode PROC(REF FILE)

VOID. They can all be used in the transput parameters of read, write or print, but not in readf, writef or printf (to be described later). The procedures are:

newline   *skip to the start of the next line (which might be the first line on the next page)*

newpage   *skip to the start of the first line on the next page*

space   *skip ahead by one character (which might cause a new line or page to be taken)*

backspace *go back one character within the current line (not from the first position in the line)*

The distinction between the space procedure and the space character can sometimes be important. For example,

     write((backspace, space))

achieves nothing, whereas

     write((backspace, " "))

wipes out the last character to have been output in the current line. Backspacing is made possible by the fact that character transput takes place line by line, with the aid of a one-line buffer held in the file variable.

7.4.2 Absolute positioning

The standard channels are initialized to start at character 1 on line 1 on page 1, and as transput proceeds, these numbers are kept up-to-date. The character position applies to the next character to be read or written. Thus, for a line length of 120 characters, the 'charnumber' can range from 1 to 121, at which point no further character is transput until a new line has been taken. This adds 1 to the line number and sets the charnumber back to 1. Similar considerations apply to lines and pages. The current position integers are given by the following procedures.

     PROC(REF FILE)INT

charnumber   =   *character position in the current line,*

line number   =   *line number in the current page,*

page number   =   *page number (in the book)*

As a simple example, the following step might be taken to prevent an impending output string from going over the end of the line.

     IF charnumber(standout) > 40 THEN newline(standout) FI

The transput position in the current line can be abruptly altered—forwards or backwards—by the procedure 'set charnumber':

     PROC(REF FILE, INT)VOID set charnumber =
        set the character position in the current line to the given INT

For example, 'set charnumber(standout, 1)' would prepare for the overwriting of the current line of output. As with 'backspace', this possibility arises from the fact that output does not, in fact, take place one character at a time, but line by line.

7.4.3 Styling of numbers for output

The standard output styles for numbers shown in Section 7.3.1 will often be found too clumsy. The accuracy of a computation may not justify printing answers to seventeen figures (a not unusual default), and the range of values may be such that the floating point notation is uncalled for. The normal way of varying these styles is to use formatting (Section 7.5). An alternative method is to convert results into character strings by means of the procedures described below. By using these in the transput parameter of 'write', this procedure's conversion of numbers to characters is by-passed. So too—since it is strings that are being output—is the mechanism by which 'write' takes a new line before printing a number which would not fit on the current line. Care must therefore be taken to prevent a number getting split across two lines, which would make it unsuitable for any subsequent formatless input.

Each of the three conversion procedures takes for its first parameter any kind of number except complex—that is, any integer or real, including short and long versions. The remaining parameters are integers and the mode of the result is STRING.

whole (x, n)

> Gives a string of ABS n characters presenting x in integer form, rounded if x is REAL. Leading zeros in all but the final digit position are replaced by spaces. If n is positive, the string includes a plus or minus sign, but if n is negative, a plus sign is omitted and *not* replaced by a space. If n is zero, a string of minimum length is produced, containing no spaces (see text for an example).

fixed (x, n, d)

> Gives a string of ABS n characters presenting x with d digits after the point. Leading zeros are replaced by spaces in all but the position immediately before the point. If n is positive, the string includes a plus or minus sign, but if n is negative, a plus sign is omitted and *not* replaced by a space. If n is zero, the minimum string containing no spaces is produced.

float (x, n, d, e)

> Gives a string of ABS n characters presenting x in floating point notation, with d digits after the point and an exponent of ABS e characters after the exponent symbol. If n is positive, the string includes a plus or minus sign for the mantissa, but if n is negative, a plus is represented by a space. If e is positive, the exponent includes a plus or minus sign (counted in e), but if e is negative, a plus sign is omitted and *not* replaced by a space (so that e works like n in 'whole').

In using any of these procedures, care should be taken to allow enough space for the expected values of x. If the length of string given is too small for the representation requested, the string is not extended. With the procedure 'whole', the string is filled with asterisks—or other local characters given by 'error char'. With the other two procedures, there may be some room for adjustment. With 'fixed', the value of d will be reduced to ensure space for the digits before the point. With 'float', if the number of digits for the exponent is insufficient, the exponent is allowed to take space from the right-hand end of the mantissa. These measures are designed to preserve as much information as possible without lengthening the string; when they fail, the string is filled with error characters.

Examples of conversions from numerical value to string are shown below. Primes are used to indicate spaces for ease of understanding.

procedure call	*STRING resulting*	
whole(12.3, 5)	´´+12	
whole(123, 4)	+123	
whole(123, 3)	***	
whole(123, −3)	123	
whole(−123, 6)	´´−123	
fixed(100/3, −6, 2)	´33.33	
fixed(100/3, −5, 2)	33.33	
fixed(−100/3, 6, 2)	−33.33	
fixed(−100/3, 5, 2)	−33.3	(d reduced)
float(100/3, 12, 4, 2)	+333.3333e−1	
float(100/3, 12, 4, 4)	+3.3333e´´+1	
float(100/3, 5, 0, −1)	+33e0	
float(100/3, 4, 0, −1)	+3e1	
float(10e10, −10, 4, −2)	´1.0000e11	
float(10e10, −10, 4, 2)	´1.000e+11	(d reduced)
float(10e10, −10, 4, 3)	´.1000e+12	

Remember that the procedures 'whole', 'fixed' and 'float' do not perform transput; for output, 'write' must be called with the string as the transput item, as in

write(("pi = ", fixed(pi, −7, 5)))

which prints 'pi = 3.14159' (without the quotes).

The special facility for obtaining a minimum length string when using 'whole' or 'fixed' with zero as the second parameter is most useful for embedding numbers in text without unsightly gaps. For example,

write(("You have only $", whole(credit, 0), " left"))

could produce outputs such as

You have only $2358072 left
You have only $2 left

7.5 Formatting

On the standard channels, formatting is obtained by use of 'readf' for input and 'writef' or 'printf' (the same procedure) for output. These procedures will not accept items of mode PROC(REF FILE)VOID, such as space or newline, but they *will* accept objects of mode FORMAT, which can do the same things and much more besides. For printed output, formatting gives a very wide degree of control over the styles and positioning of values. For input, it is mainly restrictive, forbidding values whose forms or positions do not tally exactly with the formats given in the program. For ease of explanation the subject is described here largely in terms of output, but where formatted input offers some special advantage over formatless input, this will be pointed out.

7.5.1 Pictures

To understand a format, we must first understand what is meant by a *picture*. It describes the sequence of characters which will represent or accompany some value. Suppose, for example, that we wish to print a REAL sum of French money in the form

    36,50F

Let us assume that the sum will always be positive, will not go beyond thousands of francs, and that the thousands digit (or the corresponding space) is to be printed at character position 5 in the line. After the final 'F', a new line is to be taken. All of this information is expressed in the picture

    5k 3z d s. "," 2d "F" l

(Italic type is used for formatting symbols throughout this Guide; it has no significance other than to make a clear distinction between *l* and 1.) The above picture can be read as follows:

> At character position 5 in the current line, 3 digits with leading zeros printed as spaces, then another digit in which zero is printed as 0, a suppressed decimal point, an insertion of a comma, 2 more digits, a letter F and finally a new line.

Of the eight items in this picture, the four which describe the style of the REAL value itself are

    3z d s. 2d

and these are called *frames*. The remaining items are called *insertions*. They are concerned with layout or extra characters expressed as string denotations. Remember that layout is never inserted automatically in formatted transput.

A picture need not contain any frames, though pictures without them are the exception rather than the rule. Assuming that frames are present, they must all be concerned with the transput of just one value. *No picture can describe more than one value.* It is therefore important to know just what is meant by a single value: it has one of the following modes.

basic modes	quasi-basic modes
INT*	STRING (same mode as [ ]CHAR)
REAL*	STRUCT *n* CHAR (see Section 4.4.1)
BITS*	BYTES (special case of above)
BOOL	COMPL*
CHAR	

* including short and long versions

Objects having any of the quasi-basic modes in the right-hand column are treated as single values for transput purposes. This is exceptional, as all other arrays or structures have their elements or fields counted as separate values.

7.5.2 The transput parameter with formats

A format is a list of pictures. The pictures are separated by commas and the whole, enclosed between a pair of dollar signs, is called a *format text*. Its mode is FORMAT. Being an object, it can be given an identifier, as for instance by the declaration

FORMAT f = $ 5*k* 2*zd*, 20*k* +*d*.3*d* *l* $
COMMENT
　　　This describes transput of an INT and a REAL. The integer is to start at character position 5 and have 2 digits with leading zero suppression and 1 without. The real is to start at character position 20 with a sign, then 1 digit before the point and 3 after it. Finally a new line is to be taken.
COMMENT

A format such as this could be used in various ways, such as

INT n;
REAL x;
read((n, x));
printf((f, n, x))

The format is given as one of the items in the transput parameter, not to be transput itself—which is impossible—but to control transput of the values following, here n and x. Such values need not be in one call of printf; we could equally well write

　　printf(f);　printf(n);　printf(x)

The format f remains in control throughout—but remember that to bring this about, the calls must all be of the *formatting* transput procedure. The formatless procedure 'write' (or 'print') can neither take nor make use of a format under any circumstances.

After a value has been transput, its picture is completed and the place in the format is kept. Another picture is not started until the next value is ready for transput. If, when the next picture is taken, it is found to contain only insertions, these are carried out and another picture taken. In other words, a picture without any frames is treated as though it were part of the next picture.

In the above example, the format f controls the printing of two basic items, n and x. Equally well, it could control printing of a structured item, as in

    MODE BRUSH = STRUCT(INT series, REAL width);
    BRUSH b;
    read(b);
    printf((f, b))

For transput, a structure such as b is broken down into its basic values. Here the first picture of f controls the printing of the first field of b, and the second the second.

When there are no pictures left but further values are presented for transput, the format starts again at the first picture. This is useful for dealing with arrays when all the elements are to be treated in the same way. For example, continuing with the format f already declared,

    [50]BRUSH stock;
    read(stock);
    printf((f, stock))

causes f to be cycled some 50 times. As the format includes a new line at the end of its second picture, the output will consist of two parallel columns of figures.

For a full appreciation of formatting, some knowledge of the transput mechanism is helpful. A format is held in the file variable for the channel on which it was presented—here 'standout'. It continues in use on that channel until another format is provided. This can be done at any time. Any item in a transput parameter can be a new format, and the old one is then immediately discarded, even if some of it has remained unused. The very first call of a formatted transput procedure on a given channel must always start with a format.

A format item in a transput parameter can be given as a unit whose result is a FORMAT. This is the general rule for any sort of transput item, but in practice a format will usually be given as a format text or as an identifier standing for one. If the format has an identifier, it can be associated with more than one file variable, and used independently by each. For example, the step 'read(stock)' in the last episode could have been

    readf((f, stock))

The form of data required for input would, in this case, be exactly the same as that produced on output.

7.5.3 Frames and insertions

A full list of frames and insertions is given in the accompanying Table of Formatting Codes. The frames used in any picture must, of course, be selected to suit the mode of value to be transput. For instance, a picture describing a REAL or an INT can have digit frames *d* or *z* but not character frames *a*. A character frame is used only for transput of a CHAR, and a boolean frame *b* only for a BOOL. The frames required for the various modes of value are given in Sections 7.5.3.1 to 7.5.3.3. Insertions can be interspersed in any way that may be desired. In the

Table of Formatting Codes

R = replicatable

s = suppressible

Rs	*a*	character frame
	b	boolean frame
	b( )	boolean choice frame
	c( )	integer choice frame
Rs	*d*	digit frame
s	*e*	exponent frame
	f( )	format frame
	g	general frame
	g( )	general number output frame
s	*i*	imaginary frame for complex number
R*	*k*	character position
R	*l*	new line
	n( )	dynamic replicator
R	*p*	new page
R	*q*	space character insertion
R*	*r*	radix frame (R = 2, 4, 8 or 16 only)
	s	suppression symbol
R	*x*	space
R	*y*	backspace
Rs	*z*	zero frame (digit or leading space)
s	.	decimal point frame
	+	sign frame (+ or −)
	−	sign frame (space or −)
R	"..."	literal insertion

* In this case, the word 'replicatable' is not appropriate as R has a different interpretation

following picture, for example, insertions have been placed between each separate digit of a number.

   5k d q "hundreds" *l 5k d q* "tens" *l 5k d q* "units" *l*

This could be used for printing an integer in the range 0 to 999 (there being no sign frame), and would cause 38 to be printed in the style

   0 hundreds
   3 tens
   8 units

The insertions *5k* indent each line to character position 5. The use of *q* for insertion of a space character is intended to be clearer than a space within the string insertion (e.g. " hundreds") and there is no other reason for its use in this example.

When laying out a format text, legibility is often improved by spacing out the various frames and insertions to some extent; this does not influence the machine interpretation of the format in any way.

In the Table of Formatting Codes, the frames and insertions which can be *replicated* are marked with an R. The replicator must (until Section 7.5.6) be an integer denotation. It cannot be an identifier from the program. Some examples are

> 4*d*   4 digits
> 4"!"   insertion of ! ! ! !
> 4*k*   skip to character position 4
> 4*r*   prepare to transput a BITS value in the scale of 4

The replicator 4 would normally mean '4 of the following frames or insertions'; only for *k* and *r* frames does it have a different interpretation. Certain frames can be *suppressed* by means of the suppression code *s*, which can be useful for suppressing some standard feature such as the decimal point in a real value. A different character can then be inserted in its place, as in the French money example in Section 7.5.1—which would, incidentally, work equally well for input and output. Suppressed frames on input are treated as 'make believe' characters. Thus a suppressed *a*-frame (*sa*) supplies a space without reading any character from the input data stream. A suppressed digit frame (*sd* or *sz*) supplies a zero. For example,

> INT n;
> readf((\$ *d* 3*sd* \$, n))

reads one digit, 5 say, and without reading any further characters from the actual data stream causes n to acquire the value 5000. Notice that, when replication and suppression are combined, the replicator comes first. A replicator applies to the item which follows it, which can be a frame, an insertion, a suppressed frame or a collection (Section 7.5.5).

The various insertions shown in the Table of Formatting Codes should be self-explanatory, as they all have counterparts in formatless transput. For output, there is usually nothing to choose between the *q* and *x* insertions unless backspacing has taken place. The *x* insertion moves the writing position forward without obliterating any character which may already have been written before backspacing, whereas *q* overwrites with a space character. The distinction is possibly more useful in formatted input, for *x* passes over a character without inspecting it, whilst *q* demands a space character from the input data stream. In formatted transput, every new line or page required must be taken explicitly by newline or newpage insertions *l* and *p*; automatic new lines or pages are not provided except under control of the 'general' frame.

The *general frame g* allows a value to be transput exactly as in formatless transput, and is the only frame which can be used for any value regardless of mode. When used, it must be the one and only frame in its picture, but it may of course be accompanied by insertions. This alone can make formatting worthwhile. For example,

[4]STRUCT(INT no, STRING things)s;
FORMAT f = $ *gx*, *gl* $;
readf((f, s));
printf((f, s))

would input and output data such as

+2800 screws
  +12 nuts
    +1 passports
    +3 dictionaries

with layout between the fields and elements. For output of numbers, the *g* frame can be used with parameters. It then describes the style required for an integer or real, or any long, or short version, in exactly the same way as the procedures 'whole', 'fixed' and 'float' defined in Section 7.4.3. The correspondence is

output frame	*equivalent style*
g(n)	whole(x, n)
g(n, d)	fixed(x, n, d)
g(n, d, e)	float(x, n, d, e)

To illustrate this, the two examples given in Section 7.4.3 are repeated below using printf and write for comparison.

printf(($ "pi = " *g*(−7, 5) $, pi))
write(("pi = ", fixed(pi, −7, 5)))

These produce 'pi = 3.14159' (without the quotes).

The possibility of using the *g* frame with zero as its first parameter to produce 'whole' and 'fixed' styles of minimum length for integers and reals is worth remembering, for there is no other way of achieving this effect. Thus

printf(($ "You have only $" *g*(0) *x* "left" $, credit))

is equivalent to

write(("You have only $", whole(credit, 0), space, "left"))

Apart from this, however, the styling of numbers is as easily—and perhaps more clearly—achieved by use of separate frames for each component, sign, digits, point etc, as described in the following section.

7.5.3.1 *Frames for numbers*
A printed *integer* consists only of an optional sign and digits, and yet there are many possible character representations, as the following sequence of examples shows. Each one introduces a new feature, until finally the style usually preferred is arrived at. Spaces are represented here by primes for counting purposes.

pattern of frames		*character representations of 20, −20 and 0*	
d	*fault*	*fault*	0
4*d*	0020	*fault*	0000
+4*d*	+0020	−0020	+0000
−4*d*	'0020	−0020	'0000
+4*z*	+''20	−''20	+''''
+3*zd*	+''20	−''20	+'''0
3*z*+*d*	''+20	''−20	'''+0
3*z*−*d*	'''20	''−20	''''0

Notice how, by placing the sign frame after the zero frame, we can represent a number with the sign in the most natural position, which is after the suppressed leading zeros. In any multiple *z* frame, zero suppression ceases as soon as a non-zero digit has been printed. It would start again after the intervention of a *d* frame.

A printed *real* contains a decimal point or an exponent or both. On output only, a value of mode INT can, if desired, be printed in the form of a real, as widening will take place in response to the pattern of frames given. The following sequence of examples should suffice to show the various possibilities for representing real values. Again, spaces are represented by primes for ease of counting.

pattern of frames	*character representations of 123.4 and 0.0*	
4*z*+*d*.2*d*	''+123.40	''''+0.00
4*z*+*ds*.	''+123	''''+0
+*d*.4*dez*+*d*	+1.2340e'+2	+0.0000e'+0
z−*d*.4*de*−*d*	'12.3400e'1	''0.0000e'0
4*z*+*ded*	*fault*	''''+0e0
4*z*+*de*−*z*	+12340e−2	''''+0e''

When there is an exponent, the mantissa is placed as far to the left as the pattern allows, as seen in the last example, which gives +12340e−2 rather than '+1234e−1. The purpose served by the *z* frame here is only to suppress the leading zeros of a mantissa whose value is zero.

The pattern of frames for a *complex* number is simply a pair of real patterns with an *i* frame in between. On output only, a value of mode REAL (or even INT) can be printed as a COMPL, for widening will occur in response to the format provided. The following pictures include typical patterns of frames for complex numbers, together with space insertions.

picture	*character representation of the COMPL value (12.3, 0.0)*
−*d*.4*de*−*d xix* −*d*.4*de*−*d*	'1.2300e'1'i''0.0000e'0
z−*d*.3*d si* 5*x z*−*d*.3*d*	'12.300'''''''0.000

As in previous examples, the primes represent spaces. When computing with complex numbers, the square root of -1 can appear in three different guises. In program text, I is a dyadic operator giving the COMPL value formed from its two INT or real operands. (The notation 12.3 I 0.0 is usually preferable to a structure display (12.3, 0.0), which requires a strong context.) In a data stream, the letter i, for which there may be local alternatives, is no more than a separator for the two parts of the complex number. Finally, in a format picture, *i* is the frame which controls transput of the separator i.

7.5.3.2 *Frames for characters and strings*

For transput, each of the following counts as a single value, and therefore cannot be spread over more than one picture of a format.

value	*mode*	*suggested frames*
character	CHAR	*a*
string	STRING or [ ]CHAR	*g*
character structure	STRUCT *n* CHAR	*a ... a*
or BYTES (see 4.4.1)	BYTES	*a ... a*

For any of these, the choice lies between the *a* frame suitably repeated or replicated, or the general frame *g*. If *a* frames are used, insertions can be placed between every individual character should this be wanted, but the number of characters has to be known, as the same number of *a* frames must be given. The end of a line must be foreseen, and a new line taken with an *l* insertion when required. For ordinary strings, therefore, the *g* frame is more convenient. This effects formatless transput as described in Section 7.3.2 and requires no replicator. New lines are taken automatically when required, except on input to a STRING variable.

For RS character structures, the number of characters is a fixed part of the mode, and of necessity known. It is therefore easy to use the corrrect number of *a* frames in cases where insertions between characters are required.

7.5.3.3 *Frames for booleans and BITS*

The frame for a boolean value is *b*, which must be the only frame in the picture. Occasions for using this frame are comparatively rare, as the external representations of TRUE and FALSE are the somewhat inexpressive T and F. The boolean choice frame (7.5.4) will often be preferred.

In formatted transput, a value of mode BITS is represented as an unsigned integer having radix 2, 4, 8 or 16. The pattern of frames required is the radix frame *r* preceded by the radix and followed by such *d* and *z* frames as are required. For example,

```
BITS b := 8r12;
printf(($ 2r 7zd $, b))
```

prints b as ''''1010, the primes indicating the spaces resulting from suppression of leading zeros. For a bits value, the radix frame *must* be given, and the number of digits is limited by 'bits width', which is implementation dependent.

7.5.4 Choice frames

Special frames for booleans and integers enable these values to be represented by strings of the user's own choice. The *boolean choice* frame has the form

$$b \ (\ tstring, \ fstring \ )$$

where *tstring* is the string which will represent the value TRUE and *fstring* is the string for FALSE. For example,

```
STRUCT(BOOL male, young)p : = (FALSE, TRUE);
printf(($ b("HE", "SHE")x "IS" x, b("YOUNG", "OLD") $, p))
```

would print SHE IS YOUNG. The boolean choice frame can be useful as an input format for interpreting answers to question in conversational programs. The replies YES and NO could be input by means of the frame b("YES", "NO"). Remember that, on input, the program will try to match the input characters first with *tstring* and, failing that, with *fstring*. A frame such as b("WITH", "WITHOUT") would therefore be useless for input.

There is a similar choice frame c for integers. The given strings are taken to represent 1, 2 etc up to the number of strings provided. On output, integers outside this range cause a fault to occur. The following extract shows the use of an integer choice frame to control the running of a program. The different strings are intepreted as commands which can alter the values of selected variables and re-run a given piece of the program. A steering mechanism of this kind can prove highly convenient in exploratory work at an on-line terminal.

```
REAL x, y, z;
INT n;
WHILE
    readf(( ($c ("END", " ", "x=", "y=", "z=", "RUN", "")$, n)); n > 1
DO CASE n − 1
    IN SKIP,         COMMENT ignores spaces COMMENT
        read(x),     COMMENT reads variable COMMENT
        read(y),     COMMENT reads variable COMMENT
        read(z),     COMMENT reads variable COMMENT
        unit ,       COMMENT obeys piece of program COMMENT
        read(newline) COMMENT skips mismatch COMMENT
    ESAC
OD
```

Notice the empty string as the final item in the choice frame. If no preceding string matches the input, this one surely will. The response prepares to read a further command on the next line.

7.5.5 Picture replication

The Table of Formatting Codes shows that certain frames—and all insertions—can be replicated within a picture. This section describes replication of a whole picture or collection of pictures. Although all the pictures in a format are repeated whenever the end of the format is reached, something more selective will often be needed. Consider, for example, outputting the structure

STRUCT(STRING t, [15]REAL r, INT i, j, k) s;

There are 19 values for transput, and each one needs a picture. The structure could be decomposed (t OF s, r OF s, etc.) and separate formats used for each field, but this is cumbersome. Using picture replication, a possible format for the entire structure is

$ *gl*, 15(−*d*.4*d l*) *l*, 3(−5*zd* 6*x*) 2*l* $

This sets out the string field on one line, the 15 reals on separate lines, then a blank line, the 3 integers on one line and finally 2 new lines. The new feature of the format is the use of parentheses.

A picture or sequence of pictures enclosed in parentheses is called a *collection*. A replicated collection expands into a sequence of pictures whose number is the product of the replicator and the number of pictures in the collection. Thus a picture containing a collection, such as

x 3(*a, b*) 2*x*

expands into the six pictures

*xa, b, a, b, a, b*2*x*

In its picture, a collection can be accompanied by insertions only; there can be no other collections or frames. As can be seen, the insertions preceding the collection are treated as part of the first picture of the expanded sequence, and those following it as part of the last.

When using collections, it is important to remember the significance of the brackets. Thus 5*d* is short for *ddddd*, but 5(*d*) is short for *d, d, d, d, d*. The first is a group of 5 digits from one number, but the second is 5 separate one-digit numbers. The same distinction must be made when handling strings. A typical mistake is shown in the following, which attempts to insert a space after each character in a string.

STRING ee = "Early English";
printf(($ 13(*aq*) $, ee))   ???

This is wrong because strings are single values. The format supplies 13 pictures for 13 values of mode CHAR, but what is provided for transput is one value of mode STRING. This mistake will cause a fault to occur. The following is technically correct

printf(($ *aq aq aq aq aq aq aq aq aq aq aq aq aq* $, ee))

and there is no way of shortening it with a replicator. However, the string can be broken down into its CHAR elements and an ordinary program loop employed, thus

FOR i TO UPB ee DO printf(($ *aq* $, ee[i]))

Equally well,

>   FOR i TO UPB ee DO write((ee[i], " "))

achieves the desired effect. Formatting is not compulsory!

   Replicated collections are most useful for setting out pages of figures systematically. For example.

> $ 10(5(10($z-d.2d\ 4x$)l)l)p $

lays out 10 reals per line, 5 lines per group each followed by a blank line, and 10 groups per page. The 500 pictures can then be allowed to cycle for successive pages of output.

7.5.6 Dynamic features — *n* and *f* frames

   If the amount of replication required for a frame, insertion or collection is not known when the program is being written, the replicator cannot be given as an integer denotation. A program variable cannot be used in its place unless it is bracketed and preceded by the formatting code *n*. Thus, if i is an integer variable in the program, *n*(i)*x* would insert i spaces. The general form of a dynamic replicator is

>   *n* (*series*)

where the *series* could be just a primary or it could be a whole series of steps, provided that an integer value is finally delivered as the result. Dynamic replication is used mainly for transput of arrays. For example, to transput a structure such as

>   STRUCT(STRING t, [n]REAL r, INT i, j, k)x

the format could be the same as that given in Section 7.5.5 for a similar structure, but with *n*(n) in place of 15, thus

> $ *gl*, *n*(n)($-d.4d\ l$) l, 3($-5zd\ 6x$) 2l $

   The body of a dynamic replicator is evaluated at the last possible moment, even though the format may have been given an identifier in an identity declaration. Thus

>   STRING s;
>   FORMAT f = $ *5k gl 5k n*(UPB s)"–" 2l $;
>   read(s);
>   printf((f, s))

could read in SYMPHONY OF PSALMS and print

```
SYMPHONY OF PSALMS
- - - - - - - - - - - - - - - - - -
```

Everything in a format text must be valid when actually *used*.

The other dynamic feature available in a format text is a subroutine facility. This takes the form

   $f(\ series\ )$

The *series* must deliver a FORMAT, which can then be imagined to occupy the place of the *f* construction. In its picture, the *f* construction can be accompanied by insertions only, and it cannot be replicated. As an example of its use,

```
MODE DATE = STRUCT(INT day, month, year);
MODE HOLIDAY = STRUCT(DATE start, finish);
FORMAT date = $ g(0)x,
                  c("January", "February", "March",
                    "April", "May", "June",
                    "July", "August", "September",
                    "October", "November", "December"),
                  ","x4d $;
HOLIDAY h := ((20, 8, 1968), (6, 9, 1968));
printf(($ f(date), q"to" q f(date) $, h))
```

prints

   20 August, 1968 to 6 September, 1968

As with the *n* construction, care must be taken to ensure that everything in the format text is valid when substituted and obeyed. The series in both constructions are obeyed at the latest possible moments—that is, immediately before transput of the values concerned.

7.6 Events

An event is an impasse or potential error encountered during transput, such as an attempt to input data which is not there. To the various different types of event, the transput procedures make certain standard responses, such as faulting the program or taking some action which allows the program to continue. The programmer, anticipating certain events, may wish to override the standard responses and provide some alternative courses of action. The event handling mechanism allows this to be done quite simply. The central role in this mechanism is played by the file variable for the channel concerned, and some attention must therefore be given to this first.

7.6.1 File variables and event procedures

The input procedures read and readf operate on the same channel and use 'standin' as their file variable. Similarly, write and writef (or print and printf) use 'standout'. The advantage of these standard file variables is that they are already declared and initialized before the start of the user's program. However, additional file variables are needed for extra channels of input or output, and may be needed for event handling. More general transput procedures must then be used, with an extra parameter through which the file variable (mode REF FILE) may be specified. In fact, the ordinary transput procedures can be defined in terms of the more general ones, as shown in the following table, where *tp* stands for 'transput parameter'.

implicit file variable	*explicit file variable*
read(*tp*)	get(standin, *tp*)
readf(*tp*)	getf(standin, *tp*)
write(*tp*), print(*tp*)	put(standout, *tp*)
writef(*tp*), printf(*tp*)	putf(standout, *tp*)
readbin(*tp*)	getbin(standback, *tp*)
writebin(*tp*)	putbin(standback, *tp*)

The mode FILE is not publicly defined. It is a structure whose fields consist of transput control information to which the user has no direct access. Amongst the various items held in every file variable is a set of 'event procedures', one for each type of event. Before responding to an event, the transput procedure itself calls the appropriate event procedure, which will deliver back one of two results, FALSE or TRUE. The transput procedure interprets these values in the following way.

FALSE   proceed with the standard response
TRUE   proceed as though the event had not happened

The event procedures with which a file variable is initialized all deliver FALSE (and do nothing else). A user's own event procedure might do this also, but would be more likely to apply some remedy and then deliver TRUE. An event procedure which delivers TRUE *without* applying a remedy can be disastrous, and may easily cause a spin. Installing a new event procedure in a file variable cannot be done by assignment, for the fields of the file variable are not revealed; it is done by calling a special setting up procedure with the file variable as one parameter and the event procedure as the other.

To illustrate these ideas, we shall consider one particular type of event. The 'end of page' event occurs when further transput is attempted after the end of the current page has been reached. The standard response of the transput procedure is to take a new page and simply carry on. To alter this, the following setting up procedure is called:

on page end(*file variable, event procedure*)

the mode of which is PROC(REF FILE, PROC(REF FILE)BOOL)VOID. As an exercise, consider the effect of

PROC ournewpage = (REF FILE f)BOOL: (newpage(f); TRUE);
on page end(standout, ournewpage)

As soon as a transput procedure using standout tries to output beyond the end of the current page, it will call 'ournewpage' with the parameter standout. This will take a new page on standout for itself, and deliver TRUE to prevent the transput procedure from taking a new page also. No useful purpose has been served, but 'ournewpage' could easily be embellished to include extra items of transput, such as a continuation title, at the top of each new page.

Notice that the formal parameter f is used as the file variable for transput within the event procedure, rather than standout. This is good practice when the event procedure is to affect the very channel which gave rise to the event. It enables the same event procedure to be installed in other file variables when the same response is required on a number of different channels.

On the standard channels, event procedures should be set up at the outermost level of the program, for otherwise the lifetime of the event procedure—which is limited by the ranges of any non-locals it uses—may not be long enough to cover the whole life of the file variable in which it has been installed. If the event procedure has to have a limited lifetime, it should be used only with a file variable with the same life, so that the validity of the original file variable is never endangered. For example, the following closed clause creates a local reference p which is used in the event procedure 'numberpage'. This makes numberpage invalid outside the closed clause. It must therefore not be installed in standout, but a copy of standout should be made for local use. This is easily done by one simple assignment.

```
BEGIN
    FILE tempout := standout;
    INT p := 0;
    PROC numberpage = (REF FILE f)BOOL:
    BEGIN
        put(f, (newpage, whole(p PLUSAB 1, 0), newline, newline ));
        TRUE
    END;
    on page end(tempout, numberpage);
    . . . . . .
END
```

After numberpage has been installed in tempout by the call of 'on page end', pages will of course be numbered only while output is being carried out with tempout as the file variable.

7.6.2 Types of event

The different types of event are listed below. For each one, the setting up procedure for a new event response takes the file variable as its first parameter and the new event procedure as the second, as already described in Section 7.6.1. The mode of the event procedure is given in the third column, from which it will be seen that the character event is exceptional.

type of event	setting up procedure	mode of event procedure
end of format	'on format end'	PROC(REF FILE)BOOL
end of line	'on line end'	PROC(REF FILE)BOOL
end of page	'on page end'	PROC(REF FILE)BOOL
output book full	'on physical file end'	PROC(REF FILE)BOOL
input data exhausted	'on logical file end'	PROC(REF FILE)BOOL
erroneous value	'on value error'	PROC(REF FILE)BOOL
erroneous character	'on char error'	PROC(REF FILE, REF CHAR)BOOL

These are now described in turn, with indications of how they might usefully be applied.

End of format
When the end of a format has been reached, the standard response is to start again at the first picture. A user's event procedure could set up a different format by calling putf with the new format as its transput parameter, and deliver TRUE to inhibit the standard response.

End of line
In formatted transput, any attempt to transput beyond the end of a line gives rise to a fault, and it would be unwise to alter this response. In formatless transput, the standard response is to take a new line. However, input to a STRING variable is exceptional whether formatted or not. If the end of a line is reached during input to a STRING variable, the event procedure is called and the standard response is to terminate the string and *not* take a new line. A user's event procedure could prevent the end of the line from terminating the string, as shown in the following episode. Some other string termination would, of course, become necessary.

```
FILE ownin := standin;
maketerm(ownin, ".");
PROC stringover = (REF FILE f)BOOL: (newline(f); TRUE);
on line end(ownin, stringover);
STRING s;
get(ownin, s);
. . . . . . . . .
```

The file variable is copied so that the standard response can be obtained by using 'standin' and the altered response by using 'ownin'.

End of page
The standard response is to take a new page. An example of how this response might usefully be altered is given in Section 7.6.1.

Output book full (end of physical file)
This event occurs if output is attempted after the external medium is full, and the standard response is installation dependent. If a user's event procedure delivers TRUE, the output is tried again.

Input data exhausted (end of logical file)
The standard response is installation dependent. If a user's event procedure delivers TRUE, input is attempted again. However, the event procedure might GOTO some other part of the program, thus preventing any further attempt to input non-existent data. For example,

```
PROC escape = (REF FILE f)BOOL: GOTO lab;
on logical file end(standin, escape);
. . . . . . . . . .
lab:
```

Notice that this event procedure does not deliver an explicit boolean result, as its final (and only) step is a jump. As 'lab' is non-local to the event procedure, the valid lifetime of the event procedure will be restricted to the range of 'lab'. If this is less than the whole program, a temporary file variable should be used in place of standin, as described in Section 7.6.1.

Erroneous value

The standard response to a value error is to fault the program. On input, the event can occur as a result of reading a value too large to store. If the event procedure delivers TRUE, the offending value is not used, but transput then continues normally. On output, the most likely cause of the event is incompatibility between a value and its format picture, for instance not enough digit frames or a value beyond the limits of a choice frame. The standard response is to output the value in formatless style before faulting the program. If, in RS systems, the event procedure delivers TRUE, a sequence of error characters ('error char') of appropriate length is output in place of the value, and the program is allowed to continue. For either formatted input or output, an erroneous value can mean that a frame in a picture is not appropriate for the mode of value being transput.

Erroneous character

This is an input event, and occurs whenever an unexpected character is encountered. The transput procedure calls the event procedure and supplies it with a suggestion as to the sort of character it had been expecting. The event procedure, as can be seen from the list at the beginning of this section, has an extra parameter of mode REF CHAR for this purpose. A user's event procedure can inspect the suggested character and let it stand, or it can assign a different one. The transput procedure substitutes the new character (the suggestion or its replacement) for the offending one. If the event procedure delivers FALSE, a fault is reported. If it delivers TRUE, input continues normally (if possible!). The transput procedure's initial suggestion is made as follows.

expected type of character	*suggested substitution*
boolean	F (or value of 'flop')
imaginary symbol	i
format insertion	the insertion
digit or suppressed zero	0
sign	+
point	.
exponent sign	e

As an example suppose that we anticipate some commas instead of decimal points in a data stream being input under control of a format which specifies points.

These could be corrected as follows. Notice the use of backspace to find out what the offending character actually was.

```
PROC commadec = (REF FILE f, REF CHAR sub)BOOL:
sub = "." AND (CHAR found;
                    get(f, (backspace, found));
                    found = ",");
on char error(standin, commadec)
```

7.7 Binary transput

Binary transput is used for outputting results efficiently without conversion to character form: such results are useful only for subsequent input to a program. The standard binary transput procedures 'write bin' and 'read bin' operate on one and the same channel under the control of the file variable 'standback', which is declared and initialized automatically before the start of the user's program. (There is no alternative identifier 'printbin' for binary output.) The more general binary transput procedures for use with any file variables are 'putbin' and 'getbin', which are analogous to 'put' and 'get' in character transput. Items of mode PROC(REF FILE)VOID such as newline or newpage cannot be included in a binary transput parameter.

Although the stored data is in binary form, position is still measured in character units. Transput begins at character position 1 of line 1 of page 1 and proceeds serially until repositioned. A new transput position can be chosen at any stage by calling the procedure 'set', whose mode is PROC(REF FILE, INT, INT, INT) VOID. Thus

```
set(standback, p, l, c)
```

sets the position on the standard channel to page p, line l, charnumber c. Within the current line, a new position can be chosen by means of the procedure 'set charnumber', as in character transput (7.4.2), thus

```
set charnumber(standback, c)
```

To return to the initial position, the simple procedure call

```
reset(standback)
```

can be used. This procedure, of mode PROC(REF FILE)VOID, is equivalent to 'set' with all the position integers as 1.

The current transput position can be ascertained by means of the procedures given in Section 7.4.2; thus,

```
charnumber(standback)
line number(standback)
page number(standback)
```

each deliver integers. Note that in binary transput, the position is the same for input and output. This is because they share the same channel, writing to and reading from the same book.

7.8 Extra channels

In simple tasks, the three standard transput channels usually provide all that is required. But many tasks are not simple, and require additional channels. It might be necessary, for example, to input data from several distinct sources intermittently, or prepare several output documents more or less simultaneously. It is not difficult to open extra channels, and the same technique can also be used for closing one of the standard channels and reopening it to connect it to a different 'book' (probably a filestore file in a large computing system).

To open a channel, only two steps are needed, one to declare a FILE variable and the other to initialize it. Thus, for an extra channel of character input,

```
FILE aux in;
open(aux in, "DICTIONARY", channeltype);
. . .
get(aux in, transput parameter)
```

The second parameter of 'open' is the title of a book known to the operating system. Details of how to give this and the third parameter must be sought in local documentation, as it is installation dependent. The procedure 'open' delivers an integer which is zero if the opening is successful. This result can simply be discarded if not required, as in the above extract. As the prime function of 'open' is to initialize the FILE variable, it is sensible practice to call it immediately after the variable is declared.

For an input channel, 'open' is the appropriate procedure to use because it connects the program to an existing book. For output, however, there are other possibilities. The procedure 'create' will usually be more convenient, as it does not require a book to exist beforehand. It causes the operating system to create one, and might also instruct it to print the book out at the end of the program run. The following extract shows a call of 'create'.

```
FILE out 2;
create(out 2, channeltype);
. . .
put(out 2, transput parameter )
```

Though discarded here, 'create' also delivers an integer which is zero if the procedure succeeds in its task.

Yet a third way of opening an extra channel is to call the procedure 'establish'. In addition to creating a new book, this procedure gives it a title for passing on to the operating system, and a maximum size (number of pages, lines per page and characters per line in that order). It is suitable for making a new output book which is to be kept for future use. Thus,

```
FILE special;
establish(special, "INVENTORY", channeltype, 5, 60, 120);
. . .
putf(special, $ g2l, f(f) $);
. . .
```

Again, zero is delivered by 'establish' if the call is successful.

When choosing between the three different ways of opening an extra channel, local documentation must be consulted. The procedures 'open', 'create' and 'establish' have to work in cooperation with the machine operating system, and are therefore bound to reflect any special properties or idiosyncrasies which this may have. The same applies with equal force to channel closure. The standard channels are closed automatically after the end of the user's program, but any channel can be closed in the course of a program run if it is desired to disconnect the program from one of its books. Algol 68 provides a choice of three procedures for this purpose, 'close', 'lock' and 'scratch', all of mode PROC(REF FILE)VOID. The normal procedure is 'close'; 'lock' is intended to close the channel and safeguard the contents of the book in some way, whilst 'scratch' is intended to close the channel and inform the operating system that the book is permanently finished with.

7.8.1 Internal transput

Internal transput—something of a contradiction in terms—is a form of character transput in which the external book is replaced by a character array variable in the program. This may be useful in fields of work concerned mainly with character manipulation. Internal transput is controlled by a single FILE variable for input and output, and it provides a random access facility similar to that of binary transput. In special applications, therefore, the character array can prove useful as a buffer between the program and an external book whose lines must be accessed serially.

Before an internal transput channel can be opened, a character array variable must be declared. To represent a book of 5 pages, each of 60 lines of 100 characters, a row of row of row of characters is needed, thus

    [5][60][100]CHAR book;

The channel is then opened in the usual way, but with 'associate' as the opening procedure, as in

    FILE bookmark;
    associate(bookmark, book);
    . . .

Transput to 'book' starts at page 1, line 1, charnumber 1 and proceeds serially until the transput position is set to some new position or reset to the beginning. This is done by the procedures 'set' and 'reset' described in Section 7.7 for binary transput. For example,

    CHAR c;
    set(bookmark, 3, 1, 18);
    get(bookmark, c);
    set(bookmark, 4, 1, 18);
    put(bookmark, c)

reads the character at page 3, line 1, charnumber 18 and copies it to the same position on the next page. To reproduce the whole book on an external medium, it can be output on the standard channel by

   printf (($ 60(100*al*)*p* $, book))

Notice that one line of characters, having mode [ ]CHAR, counts as a single value for formatting purposes, and can therefore be described in a single picture (100*al*). A page of characters, with mode [ ][ ]CHAR, counts as 60 values.

8 Modules

8.1 Modular compilation

The subject of this chapter lies beyond the formal Algol 68 language standard, being concerned with the RS system of compilation. This provides an extremely flexible yet secure way of dividing programs up into *modules* which can be compiled separately. To achieve continuity, selected indicators (that is, identifiers, mode names and operators) declared in one module are carried over for use in another. The declared meanings of such indicators are preserved, and the rigorous mode checking so characteristic of Algol 68 is maintained throughout.

A very small program does not need to be divided into modules. It can be compiled as a single module—though by the time it is run, the system will have added a selection of its own compiled modules to provide standard facilities needed by the user's program. As this happens automatically, the user need not be concerned.* The form of a program to be compiled without subdivision is

> PROGRAM *progtitle*
> *enclosed clause*
> FINISH

The *progtitle* is the user's own identification for the program. The first and third lines shown here and in previous chapters are the minimum formalities required by the RS compilation system.

Programs of moderate size usually fall naturally into sections, but there is still no need to make each section into a separate module; effort can be wasted by rushing into modular compilation without adequate thought. It may be best to leave aside the question of whether and how to subdivide a new program until a fairly advanced stage, when the desired overall shape and likely future of the program have become clear. For really large programs, the situation may be different, especially if the work is to be shared amongst a team of programmers. Modules may then be an obvious means of subdividing the work from the start, though eventually the boundaries may have to be adjusted and every module recompiled.

The purposes served by modules are similar in many ways to those of procedures, but on a larger scale. One type of module might consist entirely of useful procedures in a particular field of work. Once written, compiled, tested and documented, this type of module can be a real boon. A private library might consist of several of these. Another type of module might be a skeleton program for some

---

* Certain facilities, principally transput, are provided routinely for all users' programs. In special circumstances where no Algol 68 transput is required, it is possible to opt out of such provision by compiling in a 'void context', particulars of which may be found in local installation documents.

stereotyped problem in which it is only necessary to fill in certain of the gaps afresh to form a new program ready to run.

Apart from the more obvious practical advantages of modular compilation, there are hidden advantages. In order to draw up a program in modular form, interfaces must be specified and an editorial frame of mind adopted. Weaknesses and untidiness in program design may quickly become more evident and the overall work-plan can often be seen more broadly. Harder to pinpoint, but just as important, is the element of security; it is less easy to tinker with a compiled module than with a page of source text, especially as the interfaces are checked by the compilation system. Finally, modules have the effect of localizing errors, so easing the maintenance of very large programs. The underlying aim is that of Algol 68 itself: to facilitate well structured work.

8.2 Modules for declarations

A particular program may have engendered a suite of declarations considered to be of general use for future programs. Such declarations can be compiled in an independent module having the form

```
DECS decstitle :
step ; step ; . . . . . . step          (the decsbody)
KEEP keeplist
FINISH
```

The *decstitle* is the user's own identifier for the module, and the *decsbody* is a sequence of steps including the required declarations. A particular point to notice is the absence of any brackets around the decsbody, and the colon which precedes it. The decsbody is not like a formal series in a program; the final step can be a declaration, and is followed by the word KEEP. Any units obeyed in DECS modules are subject to restrictions set out later in this section, but units as steps may nevertheless be found useful in a DECS module for setting up purposes.

The *keeplist* is a list of the indicators to be retained after compilation of the DECS module for use in other modules. The indicators are separated by commas and can appear in any order. Operators must be followed by the mode(s) of operand(s) in parentheses, as shown in the example below. This ensures that under any circumstance the correct definition is kept.

```
DECS circledecs:
MODE POINT = STRUCT(REAL x, y);
MODE CIRCLE = STRUCT(POINT centre, REAL radius);
CIRCLE unitcircle = ((0.0, 0.0), 1.0);
OP* = (REAL x, CIRCLE c)CIRCLE:
        (centre OF c, x * radius OF c)
KEEP POINT, CIRCLE, unitcircle, *(REAL, CIRCLE)
FINISH
```

Once the above DECS module has been compiled and put away (for which local system documentation must be consulted), it can later be used in a PROGRAM module such as

> PROGRAM wheels
> USE circledecs
> *enclosed clause*
> FINISH

The new feature here is the USE command, which makes all the items kept by 'circledecs' available for use in the enclosed clause.

Declarations modules may themselves have USE commands (after the title and before the colon) enabling them to use objects, modes and operators whose indicators have been kept by previously compiled DECS modules. The USE command can include any number of DECS module titles, separated by commas. The types of module so far described may therefore be summarized as follows.

declarations modules	main program module
DECS *decstitle*	PROGRAM *progtitle*
[USE *uselist*] :	[USE *uselist*]
decsbody	*enclosed clause*
KEEP *keeplist*	FINISH
FINISH	

Square brackets indicate optional parts. The bridging which enables an indicator from one module to be used in another is its inclusion in the keeplist of the DECS module *and* the inclusion of this module's title in the *uselist* of the using module. Both of these conditions are essential. No module can be compiled until all the DECS modules in its USE command have been compiled. The order in which they are listed in the USE command is important only if the same indicator has been declared in more than one module and kept by each. When such a clash occurs, the definition taken is that from the module which is later in the USE command.

The user need not be concerned with the order in which the different DECS modules will be obeyed when the complete program has been assembled. Restrictions are imposed on the writing of DECS modules to prevent the order from mattering. These are:

DECS module restrictions

1 Calls of procedures and user-defined operators can appear only within routine texts.

2 References kept from other modules can be used only in routine texts, and this applies also to externally declared structures, arrays and unions containing references.

3 No step in the outermost level of a decsbody may be labelled.

The first two restrictions prevent a DECS module from altering any initializations carried out by another such module. Suppose, for instance, that a DECS module declares and initializes a variable intended for use in the main program, thus

    INT p := 400
    KEEP p

When using the module containing this extract, the main program is sure to find the variable p holding 400, as no intervening module is allowed to use it. The variable could appear in routine texts in other using modules, but by rule 1 no such routine text can be obeyed in any DECS module. It can be seen from this that the purpose of DECS modules is limited to setting the stage for a main program module.

8.3 Insertions in the main program

8.3.1 PROGRAM modules

The main program—as distinct from preliminary DECS modules—can be composed of more than one PROGRAM module. This is especially useful when developing long programs, as it enables parts of the program to be rewritten and recompiled without affecting earlier *or later* parts. The outermost PROGRAM module is written with 'holes' at which other modules are to be inserted. These in turn may have holes, but one level of nesting will often be adequate. At each hole, a keeplist must be given, to make indicators from the outer module available to the inner. The body of the inner module gives the enclosed clause to be obeyed at the hole when the program has been assembled. No result can be delivered by the inner module; communication between modules takes place by means of variables.

The holes in an outer module are named with identifiers, which must be listed in parentheses just before the module's title. In addition, the position of each hole is marked in the program by a 'HERE clause', which is a special unit of the form

    HERE *holename* (*keeplist*)

The following example shows two holes, 'bidding' and 'playing', in a module entitled 'bridge'.

    PROGRAM (bidding, playing) bridge
    BEGIN
        MODE CARD = STRUCT(. . . . . .);
        [52]CARD pack;
        . . . . . .
        HERE bidding(CARD, pack, . . .);
        . . . . . .
        HERE playing(CARD, pack, . . .);
        . . . . . .
    END
    FINISH

The keeplists at the different holes in a PROGRAM module need not be the same; the only condition is that the kept indicators should be valid, i.e. within their ranges, at the HERE clause. The names of the holes are not the titles of the modules to be inserted, so programs can be run with different inner modules without necessarily recompiling the outer module.

If an inner module is to use any of the indicators kept at the hole in the outer module, it must include in its preamble a 'context statement' of the form

CONTEXT *holename* IN *progtitle*

where *progtitle* is the title of the PROGRAM module containing the hole. For example, modules to be inserted at 'bidding' and 'playing' in the module 'bridge' could be

PROGRAM bidmodule
CONTEXT bidding IN bridge
enclosed clause
FINISH

and

PROGRAM playmodule
CONTEXT playing IN bridge
enclosed clause
FINISH

A module with a CONTEXT statement cannot be compiled until the outer module supplying the context ('bridge') has been compiled, and cannot be used in any context other than that specified.

Inner modules can use DECS modules if required, the USE command being given after the CONTEXT statement. PROGRAM modules of the types discussed so far all consist of an enclosed clause with a preamble defining the interface with other modules, and it is useful to describe such modules as 'enclosed clause' modules.

Form of an 'enclosed clause' PROGRAM module
Parts shown in square brackets are optional

PROGRAM [(*holelist*)] *progtitle*
[CONTEXT *holename* IN *progtitle*]
[USE *uselist*]
enclosed clause
FINISH

Summary
1 The CONTEXT statement makes indicators kept at the specified hole available for use in the *enclosed clause*. In all normal circumstances, an outermost module has no CONTEXT statement.

2 The *uselist* lists the titles of DECS modules whose kept indicators are required in the *enclosed clause*.

3 If clashes occur between kept indicators, the definitions taken are those of the modules mentioned latest. The kepts from DECS modules therefore take precedence over those from the CONTEXT.

Unless otherwise stated in the documentation of a particular RS system, the separate compilation of outer and inner PROGRAM modules does not perform the task of program assembly. This is effected in a *composition module*, of which the following is an example.

> PROGRAM bridgeprog
> COMPOSE bridge(bidding = bidmodule, playing = playmodule)
> FINISH

The program entitled bridgeprog is a composition formed from 'bridge' with its two holes filled by 'bidmodule' and 'playmodule', all three previously compiled. A fuller account of composition modules will be found in Section 8.5.

8.3.2 DECS modules

Inner modules written for holes in a program module may contain declarations which could usefully be relegated to their own DECS modules. If these DECS modules are to have access to the keeplist at the hole in the outer module, they must include CONTEXT statements just like the inner PROGRAM module, and will be obeyed within the HERE clause each time this is reached in the outer module. Such context-dependent DECS modules can be used only by the inner module at the specified context, and by inner modules at any 'descendent' contexts, as defined in Section 8.5.1. The form and properties of a DECS module can be summarized as follows.

Form of a DECS module

Parts in square brackets are optional

> *DECS decstitle*
> [*CONTEXT holename* IN *progtitle*]
> [USE *uselist*] :
> *decsbody*
> KEEP *keeplist*
> FINISH

Summary

1 The CONTEXT statement makes indicators in the keeplist at *holename* IN *progtitle* available for use in the *decsbody*. The DECS module itself can be used only by modules with access to this same keeplist.

2 The *uselist* lists the titles of DECS modules whose kept indicators are required in the *decsbody*. If there is a clash of meaning between kept indicators, the definition from the module latest to be mentioned applies.

3 The *decsbody* is an unbracketed sequence of steps separated by semi-colons and satisfying the three restrictions displayed in Section 8.2.

8.4 Compilation sequence and alteration of modules

No module which mentions the titles of other modules can be compiled until all of these other modules have been compiled. This fact largely determines the compilation sequence for a multi-module program. Thus, for a program with one outer and one inner module, the sequence would be

A   General DECS modules, as in Section 8.2.
B   Outer PROGRAM module, with modules A in its uselist and a HERE clause at the hole in its program.
C   Any DECS modules specifying the hole in B.
D   Inner PROGRAM module, with modules C (and possibly A) in its uselist.
E   Composition module to assemble and name the whole program.

In the composition module, no mention is made of the declarations modules, as these are incorporated automatically, without duplication.

If one module of a program is altered and recompiled, the alteration may affect other modules and necessitate their recompilation. However, modules earlier in the compilation sequence clearly need not be touched, and dependent modules need not be recompiled provided that certain properties of the altered module remain unchanged. These are: its type (DECS or enclosed clause module), its holenames and title, CONTEXT statement and keeplists. The keeplists used by dependent modules must contain exactly the same indicators as originally (in the same order), and the identifiers must have their original modes. In practice, it will be found that program corrections—as distinct from design changes—can usually be accommodated within these constraints.

8.5 Methods of composition

8.5.1 Multiple nesting

The composition of a program from its outermost module and inner modules for each of its holes has been outlined in Section 8.3.1 with the example

        PROGRAM bridgeprog
        COMPOSE bridge (bidding = bidmodule, playing = playmodule)
        FINISH

This is a special case in which the nesting is confined to a depth of one only. More generally, the rules for composing a complete program are as follows. The word COMPOSE is followed by the title of the outermost module and a parenthesized list of identities, in which each hole must be dealt with. The name of the hole is on the left of the equals sign and the title of the module to be inserted is on the right. If this module itself has holes, they are filled in exactly the same way. Thus a composition module can assemble a tree of separately compiled PROGRAM modules, such as

        COMPOSE x(hole1 = a,
                  hole2 = b(hole1 = d(hole1 = f,
                                          hole2 = g),
                             hole2 = e),
                  hole3 = c)

Notice that the same hole names can be used in different modules if desired. It is useful to describe the tree-like arrangement of *holes* in a composition in terms of descendants and ancestors. The descendants of any hole on the left of an identity are all those included in the expression on its right (so 'hole2 in x' has four descendent holes). The ancestors of a hole are all those of which it is a descendant.

When nesting extends to several levels, indicators can be handed on to successive modules by repeated keeping at descendent holes. For example, an indicator in the keeplist at 'hole2 in x' would have a range extending over the whole of module b and could therefore be included in either of b's keeplists, and so on.

8.5.2 Partial composition

This section describes a facility which is important only when a user's program requires access to two or more independent keeplists simultaneously. An explanation of how such a need might arise will be more readily understood after the technique itself has been described.

A program made up of several nested PROGRAM modules can, if desired, be assembled in stages. As an example, consider a program which could be fully composed by a composition module with the body

COMPOSE x(hole = y(hole = z))

For the present, it is reasonable to assume that module z does specify 'CONTEXT hole IN y' and that module y similarly specifies 'CONTEXT hole IN x'. This double nesting can, in fact, be composed in two separate stages. After compilation of modules x, y and z, module z can be inserted in y by

PROGRAM yz
COMPOSE y(hole = z)
FINISH

Composition modules are not permitted CONTEXT statements, but the implied context is that of the leading module. The context for yz is therefore 'hole IN x', and the composition can be completed by

PROGRAM xyz
COMPOSE x(hole = yz)
FINISH

Though serving little practical purpose, this is the simplest illustration of composition in stages.

A more interesting and fruitful method of composing xyz starts with a composition of x and y before module z appears on the scene. This is shown in

PROGRAM (h)xy
COMPOSE x(hole = y(hole = HERE h))
FINISH

Although there must be an identity for every hole in the modules of a composition, the right-hand sides need not actually fill the holes. Instead of giving the title of a module, a right-hand side can use the construction

HERE   *holename*

to name a hole in the composition module. Such holenames must be listed after the word PROGRAM, just as for ordinary enclosed clause modules. A composition module having holes is called a *partial composition*.

Although the construction HERE *holename* resembles the unit marking a hole in an enclosed clause (8.3.1), an explicit keeplist is not allowed. The implied keeplist at a hole in a partial composition is the combination of the keeplists at the hole *and all its ancestors*. In the present simple example, there is no need for module y to re-keep at its hole any indicators obtained from x's keeplist. The module to be inserted at the hole h need only specify 'CONTEXT h IN xy' to get access to the keeplists at the hole in y and the hole in x. So, after compiling z with 'CONTEXT h IN xy' in its preamble, the module

PROGRAM xyz
COMPOSE xy(h = z)
FINISH

completes the assembly of the three modules.

To see how this technique might be important, suppose that modules x and y are wholly independent—each setting the scene for some activity in a user's module z. Then module y would not specify 'CONTEXT hole IN x', as it would not need any of x's kept indicators. Indeed, module y need not have any context specified at all. But as a result of the partial composition rule already explained, module z would still have the use of kept indicators from x and y. Certain types of software package, of which graph-plotting and real-time simulation packages are examples, cannot be encapsulated in DECS modules alone. A setting up phase must precede the user's program and a clearing up phase must follow it. When using an RS Algol 68 system, such packages are written as enclosed clauses, with a hole for the user's program. To use two such packages simultaneously, the user first combines them as shown above, and then proceeds with xy in the same way as for a single package.

Appendix 1   Program graphics

Layout

The use of spaces and new lines to lay out a program clearly is essential for intelligibility. Indenting is the best way to reflect the nested structure of an Algol 68 program, and spaces should never be stinted (as in INTi=0) simply because the compiler ignores them. The following exceptions to the rule that layout is ignored by the compiler should be noted.

Spaces or new lines must not occur within any bold word or compound symbol, and new lines must not occur within identifiers or the digit sequences in integer or real denotations.

In RS systems, when a single or compound symbol is declared in an operator declaration, it must be separated by some form of layout from the identity symbol (=) which follows it. In a formula, any monadic operator starting with one of the characters $*/<=>$ must be separated from any preceding non-bold operator by some form of layout.

String denotations too long to fit on one line should be closed by a quote symbol at the end of each line, and reopened on the next. With only layout intervening, the result is treated as a single string. Within strings, spaces are significant.

Comment

Enclosed program comment can be included in any reasonable position, such as before or after semi-colons, BEGIN, END, etc. Comment can be written in three ways,

```
CO          . .  . .   . .   . . .  CO
COMMENT  . . . .   . .   . . .  COMMENT
{           . . . .   . .   . . .  }
```

The last of these possibilities makes it easy in RS systems to 'comment out' parts of a program which may themselves contain comments.

Bold words

At installations offering upper and lower case alphabets, upper case can be used for bold words and lower case for identifiers, field selectors etc., as in the present Guide. Alternatively, bold words can be enclosed in primes or preceded by a point, as shown in the following examples.

1	2	3
upper and lower	*primes*	*point*
PROGRAM mine	'PROGRAM' MINE	.PROGRAM MINE
IF random < 0.5e0	'IF' RANDOM < 0.5E0	.IF RANDOM < 0.5E0
THEN print("Head")	'THEN' PRINT("HEAD")	.THEN PRINT("HEAD")
ELSE print("Tail")	'ELSE' PRINT("TAIL")	.ELSE PRINT("TAIL")
FI	'FI'	.FI
FINISH	'FINISH'	.FINISH

Bold words declared by the user as mode names or operators can include digits, but must start with a letter. Unlike identifiers, bold words cannot include spaces. The following language words, some of which are peculiar to RS systems, must not be declared as mode names or as operator symbols.

ALIEN AT BEGIN BIOP BITS BOOL BY BYTES CASE CHANNEL CHAR CO CODE COMMENT COMPL COMPOSE CONTEXT DECS DO ELIF ELSE EMPTY END ESAC EXIT FALSE FI FILE FINISH FLEX FOR FORALL FORMAT FROM GO GOTO HEAP HERE IF IN INT IS ISNT KEEP LOC LONG MODE NIL OD OF OP OUSE OUT PRIO PROC PROGRAM REAL REF SHORT SKIP STRAIGHT STRING STRUCT THEN TO TRUE UNION USE VECTOR VOID WHILE XTYPE YTYPE

Operator symbols
An operator can be any bold word other than one of those listed above, or it can be a single or compound symbol. In RS systems, the first or only character can be chosen from the set

    + – & % ? < = > * /

The symbol can then continue, with no internal spaces, with any number of characters from the set

    < = > : * /

and is terminated when a character not in this last set (such as a space) is reached. Compound symbols are never enclosed in primes or preceded by a point like bold words.

Appendix 2   Basic modes and coercions

SHORT and LONG   For brevity, one lengthened mode only is included for the modes INT, REAL, COMPL and BITS in the list which follows. In RS Algol 68 systems, there can be up to four variants in each case, which must include the standard mode and the SHORT and LONG variants. The remaining variant can be either SHORT SHORT or LONG LONG. Appendix 4 gives examples for particular implementations. The length of a mode cannot be altered by coercion, but only by the operators LENG and SHORTEN (Appendix 3). For values of 'max int', 'long max int' etc., see Appendix 4.

INT

Integer denotations, such as 0, 5, 005, 1234567 or 1 234 567 range in value from 0 to 'max int', there being no denotation for a negative number. (The minus sign in a program is an operator, except in strings and in the exponent part of a real denotation.) In strong contexts, INT can widen to REAL.

LONG INT etc.

Denotations range from 0 to 'long max int', and must include LONG, for example LONG 0, LONG 123456789. In strong contexts, LONG INT widens to LONG REAL.

REAL

A real denotation must include a decimal point or an exponent or both, as for example

0.5,   50e−2,   50.0e−2,   .05e1,   .005e+2

The largest real value that can be stored is machine dependent, and given by 'max real'. In strong contexts, REAL widens to COMPL.

LONG REAL etc.

The denotation for a long real value is LONG followed by a number containing a decimal point, exponent, or both, as for a REAL. The largest long real value that can be stored is given by 'long max real'. In strong contexts, LONG REAL widens to LONG COMPL.

COMPL

The mode for a complex number. Although equivalent to a STRUCT(REAL re, im), an object of mode COMPL can be regarded as a single value (and is, in fact, so treated in formatted transput). It has no denotation of its own. In strong contexts, a COMPL can be expressed by a structure display, but in other contexts it is denoted as a pair of INT or REAL values separated by the dyadic operator I. Thus

COMPL c1 = (2.4, 3.6);
COMPL c2 = 2 * 1.2 I 1.8

are equal constants.

LONG COMPL etc.   A long complex value can be expressed, in strong contexts, as a structure display containing two LONG REAL values (to which LONG INT values would be widened), or, in any contexts, by a pair of LONG INT or LONG REAL values separated by the dyadic operator I. For example, with x and y as ordinary REAL values,

LONG COMPL z0 : = LONG 0;
LONG COMPL z : = (LENG x, LENG y);
LONG COMPL cc1 = (LONG 2.4, LONG 3.6);
LONG COMPL cc2 = LONG 2 * LENG x I LENG y

BITS   Bits values, consisting of 'bits width' binary digits, are denoted as integers to radix 2, 4, 8 or 16. Thus

2r11011, 4r123, 8r33 and 16r1b

all represent the same value. The letters a to f are used for the hexadecimal digits from 10 to 15. In strong contexts, BITS widens to [ ]BOOL.

LONG BITS etc.   Long bits values, consisting of 'long bits width' binary digits, are denoted to radix 2, 4, 8 or 16 preceded by LONG, thus

LONG 2r11011, LONG 4r123, LONG 8r33,
LONG 16r1b

In strong contexts, LONG BITS widens to [ ]BOOL.

BOOL   The two boolean values have denotations TRUE and FALSE.

CHAR   The denotation for a character is the character in quotes, e.g. "A", except that the denotation for the quote character itself consists of four consecutive quotes (""""), not three. A space character can be denoted either as a space in quotes or, if preferred, by the CHAR constant 'blank', thus

CHAR c : = blank

The set of available characters is implementation dependent, and the largest absolute value is given by 'max abs char'.

STRUCT *n* CHAR   This family of modes, in which *n* is an integer denotation and a *part of the mode*, is an RS language extension. The denotation for a character structure is a sequence of *n* characters enclosed in a pair of quote symbols, provided that *n* is greater than 1. Thus, "UNESCO" is a STRUCT 6 CHAR. Though not strictly a basic mode, a character structure is treated as a single value in formatted transput. In strong contexts and in operand positions, character structures coerce to STRING.

BYTES

In RS systems, this mode is defined as STRUCT *n* CHAR, where *n* is 'bytes width' (e.g. 4 if there are four characters to a machine word). There are no LONG BYTES etc. in RS systems, though equivalents may be defined in local installation libraries. In strong and operand contexts, BYTES is coerced to STRING.

STRING

This mode is [ ]CHAR, but REF STRING is REF FLEX [ ]CHAR. In formatted transput, a STRING is treated as a single value. From a formal standpoint, in RS systems a sequence of characters in quotes denotes a character structure (see above), but as this is coerced to STRING in strong and operand contexts, use of the phrase 'string denotation' is reasonable.

FORMAT

For details of this mode, see Section 7.5.

Mode changes which take place when an object is subjected to coercion are classified as follows.

type of coercion	change of mode	text reference
dereferencing	removal of initial REF	1.3
deproceduring	removal of initial PROC	5.5
uniting	enclosure in UNION( )	6.8
widening	*see list of modes above*	
rowing	introduction of [ ]	4.3.2
voiding	change to VOID	5.5

The table below shows which types of coercion are applied in the three most important kinds of context. A strong context is one in which the required mode is known.

strong context	operand context	left-hand side of assignment
dereferencing	dereferencing	
deproceduring	deproceduring	deproceduring
uniting	uniting	
widening		
rowing		
voiding		

If more than one type of coercion is needed to reach the final mode, deproceduring and dereferencing take place first of all, and can be applied repeatedly. The remaining types of coercion take place in the order shown. In RS systems, the additional coercion of a character structure (and hence BYTES) to STRING, which can take place in string and operand contexts, is applied before uniting.

Appendix 3 Standard procedures and operators

Preliminary notes

1 Transput

The standard transput procedures, fully described in Chapter 7, are not included in this Appendix.

2 Modes of number

In operator specifications, the word 'number' means an INT, REAL or COMPL in any length variation.

3 Lengths of INT, REAL, COMPL and BITS

Arithmetic can be carried out with numbers of various lengths. In RS systems, the length variations are limited to SHORT INT, INT, LONG INT and either SHORT SHORT INT or LONG LONG INT. Similarly for REAL and COMPL. There are corresponding lengths for BITS. Although the different length modes such as REAL and LONG REAL are all distinct, and cannot be coerced to each other, the actual lengths of values may not all be different. This is implementation dependent, and some further details are given in Appendix 4.

The repertoire of mathematical procedures is repeated for each length regime by a systematic change to the identifiers, wherever appropriate. Thus 'short sqrt' has mode PROC(SHORT REAL)SHORT REAL. The symbols for operators, on the other hand, are the same for operands of different lengths. For example, + between a LONG INT and a LONG REAL gives a LONG REAL result, and / between two SHORT INT operands gives a SHORT REAL quotient. Unless specified to the contrary (see note 4), different lengths cannot be mixed in one procedure or operator.

4 Italic printing of the mode *INT* signifies that no length variations apply. For example, the right operand of the exponentiation operator ∗∗ has mode *INT* for all lengths of the left operand and result. The same remark applies to the bits-handling operators SHL and SHR.

5 Priority of operators

The priority of each operator is given alongside the operator or group of operators. Priorities 1 to 9 apply to dyadic operators. Priority 10 indicates a monadic operator.

Length changing

LENG	10	Converts any number or BITS value to one size longer or
SHORTEN		shorter.

Program termination

stop   Used as a step in a program, this escapes to the end of the program. In RS systems, the mode of 'stop' is PROC VOID.

Mathematical constant

pi   The REAL circular constant.
(Also 'short pi', 'long pi', etc.)

Mathematical functions

·sqrt   Standard arithmetical functions of mode PROC(REAL)
exp   REAL.
ln

cos   Standard trigonometric functions of mode PROC(REAL)
sin   REAL.
tan

arc cos   Inverse trigonometric functions of mode PROC(REAL)
arc sin   REAL: the results are in the ranges 0 to pi (for arc cos), and
arc tan   − pi/2 to + pi/2 (for arc sin and arc tan).

General arithmetic operators

+ −	6	Plus and minus between any numbers. The mode of results is that of the (wider of the) operands. Thus, integer + integer gives integer, and integer + real gives real.
	10	Plus and minus can also be used monadically.
* /	7	Times and divide between any numbers. Integer times integer gives INT result. If either operand is COMPL, result is COMPL. All other results are REAL.
**	8	Exponentiation; raises the left operand to the *INT* power of the right. The mode of result is that of the left operand, which can be any number.
ABS	10	Absolute value (modulus) of any number. The mode of result is that of the operand, except for COMPL operand, which gives a REAL result.
SIGN	10	Applied to INT or REAL, gives the *INT* result +1 for positive operand, 0 for zero operand and −1 for negative operand.
ROUND	10	Applied to a REAL, gives the nearest INT.
ENTIER	10	Applied to a REAL, gives the largest INT less than or equal to the REAL, e.g. ENTIER −2.1 gives −3.

Integer arithmetic

OVER	7	Between INT operands, gives the INT quotient, e.g. 12 OVER 5 gives 2. For negative operand(s), the absolute value of the quotient is that which would be obtained from the absolute values of the operands, e.g. (-12) OVER 5 gives -2.
MOD	7	Between INT operands, n MOD d gives the INT in the range $(0, ABS\ d - 1)$ obtained by adding or subtracting a multiple of d from n. Thus, (-12) MOD 5 gives 3.
ODD	10	Applied to an INT, gives TRUE if the integer is odd, otherwise FALSE.

Complex arithmetic

The mode COMPL is defined as STRUCT(REAL re, im)

RE	10	Applied to a COMPL value z, gives the result 're OF z'.
IM	10	Applied to a COMPL value z, gives 'im OF z'.
I	9	Between INT or REAL operands in any combination, gives the COMPL whose re field is the left operand and im field the right operand.
ARG	10	Applied to a COMPL, gives the REAL argument (i.e. phase angle) in the range $(-pi, pi)$.
CONJ	10	Applied to a COMPL value (x, y), gives the conjugate COMPL value $(x, -y)$.

Arithmetical comparison

= /=	4	Equals and not equals between any two numbers, giving BOOL result.
< <= > >=	5	Less than, less than or equal, greater than, greater than or equal between INT or REAL operands in any combination, giving BOOL result.

Arithmetical assignment

PLUSAB	1	x PLUSAB y means x := x + y, where x is a REF to any number and the mode of y must be such that x + y is suitable for assignment to x. For example, if the left operand is REF INT, the right operand cannot be REAL. The result of the operation is the result of the assignment.
MINUSAB	1	x MINUSAB y means x := x − y and similar remarks apply.
TIMESAB	1	x TIMESAB y means x := x ∗ y and similar remarks apply.

DIVAB	1	x DIVAB y means x : = x/y, where x must be REF REAL or REF COMPL and y can be any number of a suitable mode.
OVERAB	1	n OVERAB d means n : = n OVER d, where n is REF INT and d is INT.
MODAB	1	n MODAB d means n : = n MOD d, where n is REF INT and d is INT.

Random number generation

random	Successive calls of this PROC REAL give a repeatable sequence of statistically independent pseudo-random numbers uniformly distributed in the range $0.0 \leqslant random < 1.0$.
next random	Successive calls of this PROC(REF INT)REAL with the consistent use of some integer variable v as parameter produce a repeatable sequence of random numbers similar to that of 'random' but starting at a point which depends on the integer initially assigned to v.
last random	This REF INT is initialized to ROUND(maxint/2) and is used by 'random' which is defined by

PROC random = REAL: next random(last random)

Operations on booleans

NOT	10	Gives TRUE if the operand is FALSE and vice versa.
AND	3	Gives TRUE if both operands are TRUE, otherwise gives FALSE.
OR	2	Gives TRUE if at least one operand is TRUE, otherwise gives FALSE.
ANDTH	3	(optimized boolean operator in RS systems) Similar to AND, but if the left operand is FALSE, the right operand is not evaluated and the result is FALSE.
OREL	2	(optimized boolean operator in RS systems) Similar to OR, but if the left operand is TRUE, the right operand is not evaluated and the result is TRUE.
= / =	4	Equals and not equals for boolean operands, giving boolean result.
ABS	10	Gives 1 if the operand is TRUE, otherwise gives 0, i.e. converts a BOOL to an *INT*.

Bounds of arrays

| LWB | 10 | Applied to a row, gives the lower bound as an *INT*; for arrays of more than one dimension, gives the lower bound of the first dimension as an *INT*. |

UPB	10	Similar to the above, giving the upper bound.
LWB	8	n LWB p, where n is an *INT* and p an array, gives the *INT* lower bound of the nth dimension of p. For n = 1, the monadic version is an alternative.
UPB	8	Similar to the above, giving the upper bound.

Character and string handling

The mode STRING is equivalent to [ ]CHAR, and REF STRING to REF FLEX [ ]CHAR.

The number of characters in a BYTES is implementation dependent; in RS systems, there are no SHORT or LONG versions of BYTES.

ABS	10	Applied to a CHAR, gives the equivalent internal integer of mode *INT*. (Implementation dependent)
REPR	10	Applied to an *INT*, gives the corresponding CHAR, i.e. the converse of ABS.
= / =	4	Equals and not equals between operands of mode CHAR, BYTES or STRING in any combination, giving BOOL result.
< < = > > =	5	Less than, less than or equal, greater than, greater than or equal between operands of mode CHAR, BYTES or STRING in any combination, giving BOOL result. IF c and d are characters, c < d means ABS c < ABS d

When comparing sets of characters, successive characters from each set are compared until a decision is made (on the basis of ABS values) or the lesser set is exhausted; thus "A" < "AA" is TRUE.

+	6	Between two operands of mode CHAR or STRING, gives their concatenation with mode STRING and lower bound 1. For example, "A" + "BC" gives "ABC".
*	7	One operand must be a CHAR or STRING, and the other must be an *INT*. The result is a STRING, with lower bound 1, consisting of the given character(s) replicated the given number of times. Thus 3 * "ABC" gives "ABCABCABC".
PLUSAB	1	x PLUSAB y means x : = x + y, where x is a REF STRING and y is a CHAR or STRING. The result of the operation is x.
PLUSTO	1	x PLUSTO y means y : = x + y, where y is a REF STRING and x is a CHAR or STRING. The result of the operation is y.
TIMESAB	1	x TIMESAB y means x : = x * y, where x is a REF STRING and y is an *INT*. The result of the operation is x.

ELEM	7	n ELEM b, where n is an *INT* and b is a BYTES, gives the nth character of b. In RS systems, this can also be expressed as b[n], with mode CHAR.
bytes pack		This PROC(STRING)BYTES converts a STRING of no more than 'bytes width' characters into a BYTES value. If the STRING contains fewer characters than a BYTES, it is padded on the right with null characters (Appendix 4).
char in string		This PROC(CHAR, REF *INT*, STRING)BOOL finds whether a given CHAR is present in a given STRING, and produces the corresponding BOOL result. If the result is TRUE, the subscript of the first occurrence of the CHAR in the STRING is assigned to the REF *INT*.
whole fixed float		These three procedures convert numbers into string representations, as described in Section 7.4.3.

Bits handling

A value of mode BITS consists of 'bits width' TRUE's and FALSE's corresponding to binary digits 1 and 0 internally.

ABS	10	Applied to a BITS value, gives the equivalent INT.
BIN	10	Applied to an INT value, gives the equivalent BITS.
NOT	10	Applied to a BITS value, gives the BITS value with each binary digit reversed.
AND	3	Between two BITS operands, gives the BITS obtained by applying AND to each digit regarded as a BOOL.
OR	2	Between two BITS operands, gives the BITS obtained by applying OR to each digit regarded as a BOOL.
SHL	8	b SHL n shifts the BITS b to the left by *INT* n places. Binary digits are lost on the left and 0's (FALSE's) introduced on the right.
SHR	8	b SHR n shifts the BITS b to the right by *INT* n places. Binary digits are lost on the right and 0's (FALSE's) introduced on the left.
= /=	4	Equals and not equals between BITS values, giving BOOL result.
<= >=	5	If b1 and b2 are two BITS values, b1 <= b2 gives TRUE if each TRUE in b1 is also TRUE in b2.
ELEM	7	n ELEM b gives nth binary digit of b as a BOOL. The operand modes are *INT* and BITS.

bitspack

This PROC([ ]BOOL)BITS converts a [ ]BOOL having not more than 'bitswidth' elements to a BITS value, padding with 0's (FALSE's) on the left.

List of standard operator symbols and their priorities
(Alternative representations are given in parentheses)

+	10, 6	LENG	10
−	10, 6	LWB	10, 8
*	7	MINUSAB (−:=)	1
/	7	MOD (%*)	7
** (UP)	8	MODAB (%*:=)	1
< (LT)	5	NOT	10
<= (LE)	5	ODD	10
> (GT)	5	OR	2
>= (GE)	5	OREL	2
= (EQ)	4	OVER (%)	7
/= (NE)	4	OVERAB (%:=)	1
ABS	10	PLUSAB (+:=)	1
AND	3	PLUSTO (+=:)	1
ANDTH	3	RE	10
ARG	10	REPR	10
BIN	10	ROUND	10
CONJ	10	SHL (UP)	8
DIVAB (/:=)	1	SHORTEN	10
ELEM	7	SHR (DOWN)	8
ENTIER	10	SIGN	10
I (+*)	9	TIMESAB (*:=)	1
IM	10	UPB	10, 8

Appendix 4 Particular RS implementations

Typical features permitted to vary from one Algol 68 system to another are widths and lengths of numerical values, and certain representations which depend on the character set provided by the hardware. Particulars are given below for ICL 2900 and Honeywell Multics; the same for DEC Vax and other RS implementations can be had from the Information Officer, SWURCC, University of Bath, Claverton Down, Bath BA2 7AY, England.

Algol 68 for ICL 2900 series

Integers

INT	largest value:	INT max int $=2**31-1$
	decimal digits:	INT int width $= 10$
LONG INT	largest value:	LONG INT long max int $= 2**63-1$
	decimal digits:	INT long int width $= 19$

SHORT INT values have the same length as INT, and LONG LONG INT the same length as LONG INT. For the 2900, therefore, the Algol 68 integer constant 'int shorths' (meaning the number of distinct lengths which are standard or shorter) is 1, and 'int lengths' (the number of distinct lengths which are standard or longer) is 2.

Reals

SHORT REAL   smallest positive value: 5.4e−79 approx
                largest value:
                     SHORT REAL short max real = 7.2e75 approx
                smallest value which can meaningfully be added to 1:
                     SHORT REAL short small real = 9.5e−7 approx
                decimal digits:
                     INT short real width = 8, short exp width = 2

REAL   smallest positive value: 5.4e−79 approx
                largest value:
                     REAL max real = 7.2e75 approx
                smallest value which can meaningfully be added to 1:
                     REAL small real = 2.2e−16 approx
                decimal digits:
                     INT real width = 17,   exp width = 2

LONG REAL   smallest positive value: 5.4e−79 approx
                largest value:

LONG REAL long max real = 7.2e75 approx
smallest value which can meaningfully be added to 1:
LONG REAL long small real = 3.1e−33 approx
decimal digits:
INT long real width = 34,   long exp width = 2

LONG LONG REAL values have the same length as LONG REAL. The integer
constant 'real shorths' is 2, and 'real lengths' is 2.

Bits values

BITS   number of separate bits: INT bits width = 32

LONG BITS   number of separate bits: INT long bits width = 64

SHORT BITS values have the same width as BITS, and LONG LONG BITS the
same as LONG BITS. The integer constant 'bits shorths' is 1, and 'bits lengths' is 2.

Bytes values

For the 2900, the mode BYTES is defined as STRUCT 4 CHAR (i.e. bytes
width = 4). There are no modes SHORT BYTES, LONG BYTES or LONG
LONG BYTES.

Characters

The value of the integer constant 'max abs char' is 255, which signifies that the
operator REPR can be applied to any integer in the range 0 to 255 to form an
object of mode CHAR. Only a selection of these are actual printing characters.
The set of printing characters is given, along with the corresponding ABS values, in
the (EBCDIC) table below.

space	64	>	110
[	74	?	111
.	75	grave accent	121
<	76	:	122
(	77	£	123
+	78	@	124
!	79	acute accent	125
&	80	=	126
]	90	"	127
dollar	91	a–i	129–137
*	92	j–r	145–153
)	93	~	161
;	94	s–z	162–169
circumflex	95	{	192
−	96	A–I	193–201
/	97	}	208
bar	106	J–R	209–217
,	107	\	224
%	108	S–Z	226–233
underscore	109	0–9	240–249

The various constants of mode CHAR are defined as follows:

CHAR blank = REPR 64   CO the space character CO,
        null character = REPR 64,
        error char = "*",
        flip = "T", flop = "F"

In output data streams, the boolean values TRUE and FALSE are represented by
T and F; in input, T, Y, t or y are acceptable for TRUE and F, N, f or n for FALSE.
In output, the exponent of a real value is indicated by E, and the imaginary part of
a complex value by I; in input, upper or lower case letters may be used.

Limits for identifiers and character structures
For distinguishing between identifiers, only the first 32 non-space characters are
inspected.
    There is an absolute upper limit of 65 536 characters for the RS character
structure modes.

Representation of bold words
Bold words can be represented in any of the three ways described in Appendix 1,
the compiler determining the system in use from the first character of the module
heading. With system 2, in which bold words are enclosed between primes (acute
accents), or system 3, in which bold words are preceded by point, lower case letters
can only be used within strings or comments.

Algol 68 for Honeywell Multics

Integers
INT	largest value:	INT max int $= 2**35 - 1$
	decimal digits:	INT int width $= 11$
LONG INT	largest value:	LONG INT long max int $= 2**71 - 1$
	decimal digits:	INT long int width $= 22$

SHORT INT values have the same length as INT, and LONG LONG INT the
same length as LONG INT. For Multics, therefore, the Algol 68 integer constant
'int shorths' (meaning the number of distinct lengths which are standard or shorter)
is 1, and 'int lengths' (the number of distinct lengths which are standard or longer)
is 2.

Reals
REAL	smallest positive value: 2.9e–39 approx
	largest value:
	REAL max real $= 1.7e38$ approx
	smallest value which can meaningfully be added to 1:
	REAL small real $= 1.5e-8$ approx
	decimal digits:
	INT real width $= 9$, exp width $= 2$

LONG REAL   smallest positive value: 2.9e–39 approx
                           largest value:
                                LONG REAL long max real = 1.7e38 approx
                           smallest value which can meaningfully be added to 1:
                                LONG REAL long small real = 2.2e–19 approx
                           decimal digits:
                                INT long real width = 20,   long exp width = 2

SHORT REAL values have the same length as REAL, and LONG LONG REAL the same length as LONG REAL. The integer constant 'real shorths' is 1, and 'real lengths' is 2.

Bits values

BITS   number of separate bits: INT bits width = 36

LONG BITS   number of separate bits: INT long bits width = 72

SHORT BITS values have the same width as BITS, and LONG LONG BITS the same width as LONG BITS. The integer constant 'bits shorths' is 1, and 'bits lengths' is 2.

Bytes values

For Multics, the mode BYTES is defined as STRUCT 4 CHAR (i.e. bytes width = 4). There are no modes SHORT BYTES, LONG BYTES or LONG LONG BYTES.

Characters

The value of the integer constant 'max abs char' is 511, which signifies that the operator REPR can be applied to any integer in the range 0 to 511 to form an object of mode CHAR. Only a selection of these are actual printing characters. The set of printing characters is given, along with the corresponding ABS values, in the (ASCII) table below

space	32	;	59
!	33	<	60
"	34	=	61
hash	35	>	62
dollar	36	?	63
%	37	@	64
&	38	A–Z	65–90
acute accent	39	[	91
(	40	\	92
)	41	]	93
*	42	circumflex	94
+	43	underscore	95
,	44	grave accent	96
–	45	a–z	97–122
.	46	{	123
/	47	bar	124
0–9	48–57	}	125
:	58	~	126

The various constants of mode CHAR are defined as follows:

CHAR   blank – REPR 32   CO the space character CO,
        null character = REPR 32,
        error char = "∗",
        flip = "t", flop = "f"

In output data streams, the boolean values TRUE and FALSE are represented by t and f; in input, t, y, T or Y are acceptable for TRUE and f, n, F or N for FALSE. In output, the exponent of a real value is indicated by e, and the imaginary part of a complex value by i; in input, upper or lower case letters may be used, and the reverse solidus (reverse oblique stroke, REPR 92) is also acceptable for indicating an exponent.

Limits for identifiers and character structures
For distinguishing between identifiers, only the first 32 non-space characters are inspected.

There is an upper limit of 1 044 480 characters for the RS character structure modes.

Representation of bold words
The normal system is upper case for bold words and lower case for identifiers, as used in this Guide and described in Appendix 1 as system 1. However, it is possible to opt for the use of system 2, in which bold words are enclosed between primes (acute accents), or system 3, in which bold words are preceded by point. For each of systems 2 and 3 there are two options, upper case throughout—useful for cards—or lower case throughout. Within strings and comments, both alphabets can always be used.

Glossary

References in parentheses are to Sections in the Guide. For syntactically significant terms, the general class to which they belong (primary, expression or unit) is given along with the reference.

array (4) a group of elements all of the same mode, from which one element or a subset can be picked out dynamically by an indexer; the mode of a one-dimensional array (row) begins with [ ], a two-dimensional array (row row) with [,] and so on.

assignment (*unit*, 2.4) a group of the type *expression* : = *unit*, which assigns the result of the *unit* to the reference given by the *expression*; after the act of assignment has been carried out, the reference is taken as the result.

balancing (3.4.3) coercing of results from different branches of a conditional or case clause to the same mode.

book (7.1) figurative term for a source or sink of external data connected to a program by a transput channel; position in a book is defined by a page, line and character number.

bound (4.1) either of the two extreme values of a subscript; each dimension of an array has an upper and a lower subscript bound.

case clause (*primary*, 3.4.2) a clause enclosed by CASE and ESAC, in which a computed integer determines which of two or more units to obey.

cast (*primary*, 2.3.1) a construction of type *mode enclosed clause* which puts the *enclosed clause* into a strong context, coercing it to deliver a result of the given *mode*.

channel (7.1) a pathway for transput; a type of peripheral device as seen by the Algol 68 program.

character structure (4.4.1) the special RS mode STRUCT *n* CHAR of a string denotation, where *n* is an integer denotation giving the number of characters; a character structure is coercible to [ ]CHAR in strong contexts and in operand positions.

closed clause (*primary*, 3.2) the simplest type of enclosed clause, a series in parentheses or between BEGIN and END. [To enhance the distinction between 'closed' and 'enclosed' clause, the phrase 'simple closed clause' is preferred in the present Guide.]

coercion (Appendix 2) substitution of an object by one of a related mode to suit the context; the types of coercion are dereferencing, deproceduring, widening, rowing, uniting and voiding.

collateral (*primary*, 2.3.1) an enclosed clause consisting of units separated by commas and enclosed in parentheses; collaterals are used mainly for displaying elements of an array or fields of a structure, and must occupy strong contexts.

collection (7.5.5) a sequence of pictures enclosed in parentheses for the purpose of replication in a format.

composition (8.5) describes a type of PROGRAM module used for nesting PROGRAM modules one within another to form a complete program.

conditional (*primary*, 3.4.1) a clause enclosed by IF and FI, in which a computed boolean determines which of two series to obey.

conformity clause (*primary*, 6.8.1) a clause enclosed by CASE and ESAC, in which the current mode of a united object determines which of a number of units to obey.

declaration (2.1) a step which introduces and defines a new identifier (variable d~ or identity d~), a new mode name (mode d~), a new operator definition (operator d~) or defines the priority of a dyadic operator (priority d~).

denotation (*primary*, Appendix 2) a value explicitly represented in a program, such as the integer 3, real number 2.4e6, character "A" or boolean TRUE.

deproceduring (5.5) the coercion in which a parameterless procedure is replaced by its result, i.e. the procedure is obeyed.

dereferencing (1.3) the coercion in which a reference is replaced by the object referred to; dereferencing takes place automatically in contexts where references are unacceptable.

dimension (4.1) the domain of an array subscript; a simple row has one dimension, a rectangular array two, etc.

dimensionality (4.1) the number of dimensions of an array, which is the number of subscripts required to pick out one element.

dyadic (2.3.2) taking two operands; dyadic operators have binding priorities from 1 (weakest) to 9 (strongest); in RS systems, the priority of a new dyadic operator is assumed to be 1 unless some other priority has been declared; see also 'monadic'.

element (1.2) an individual component of an array.

enclosed clause (*primary*, 3) any of the following bracketed constructions: simple closed clause, conditional, case clause, conformity clause, loop or collateral.

enquiry clause (3.5) the clause between IF and THEN, CASE and IN, or WHILE and DO, in which no labels can be set; in this Guide, the term 'series' is preferred.

event (7.6) an impasse or potential error encountered during transput.

expression (*unit*, 2.3) that class of unit which is a primary or a selection or a formula; the term also includes generators and NIL.

field (1.2) part of a structure which can be picked out by use of a selector (qv).

file variable (7.1) a variable of the hidden mode REF FILE holding control information for transput on a particular channel; the file variables for the three standard channels are 'standin', 'standout' and 'standback' (character input, character output and binary transput respectively).

flexible array variable (4.3.4) a variable to which arrays of different sizes can be assigned; as an example, a STRING variable (having mode REF FLEX [ ]CHAR) can accommodate strings of different lengths.

format text (*primary*, 7.5) a description of the character representation and layout of a sequence of values to be transput; a format text consists of pictures separated by commas and enclosed between a pair of dollar signs.

formula (*expression*, 2.3.2) an expression consisting of primaries and selections acted on by monadic and/or dyadic operators.

frame (7.5) a component of a picture in a format text; a frame describes a part or the whole of one value, but not its position.

generator (*expression*, 3.2.2) the expression LOC *mode* or HEAP *mode* which, whenever obeyed, generates local or heap space for an object of the given *mode* and gives as its result the reference.

heap (3.2.1) a domain of store used for off-stack allocations of working space; heap space is not released whilst there remains any means of accessing it.

hole (8.3) a gap in a PROGRAM module, marked by a HERE construction, at which a separately compiled PROGRAM module can be inserted.

identifier (*primary*, 2.2) a sequence of letters and digits starting with a letter (spaces being ignored) declared to represent an object.

identity declaration (2.2.2) a step of the type *mode identifier = unit*; the *unit* is evaluated to produce an object of the given *mode*, and the *identifier* is then taken to represent this object.

identity relation (*unit*, 6.6.2) the test *expn1* IS *expn2* or *expn1* ISNT *expn2* for the equivalence or non-equivalence of two references delivered by given expressions; for use as a boolean operand an identity relation must be bracketed.

indexer (4) a square-bracketed construction placed after an array to produce a slice of the array; within the square brackets there must be one subscript or trimmer (possibly empty) for each dimension of the array, separated by commas.

indicator (8) an identifier, mode name or operator symbol; an item in a keeplist, in which operator symbols are followed by the mode(s) of operand(s).

jump (*unit*, 3.5) a step of the type GOTO label, which alters the normal sequence of the program; a jump is useful as a means of escape, e.g. from an event procedure.

keeplist (8.2) a list of source-text indicators, separated by commas, to be retained after compilation for use in some other module; operators in a keeplist must be followed in parentheses by their operand modes.

label (3.5) a program position marker, having the form of an identifier set in front of a unit in a series (label: unit) and used in a jump (qv); after a labelled unit, no later steps in the series can be declarations.

length (Appendix 3) the mode variant which determines the amounts of storage space allowed for integer, real, complex and bits values; in RS systems there are four sizes of each, e.g. for integers SHORT INT, INT, LONG INT and (implementation dependent) one or other of SHORT SHORT INT and LONG LONG INT; the amounts of space for the four distinct modes are implementation dependent and not necessarily all different.

loop (*primary*, 3.3) an enclosed clause consisting of a series between DO and OD to be obeyed repeatedly under the control of a preamble of five optional parts, FOR *identifier* FROM *unit* BY *unit* TO *unit* WHILE *series* (default values 1, 1, infinity, TRUE).

mode (1) the classification of an object; modes are divided into the types simple, array, structure, reference, procedure and union.

mode declaration (6.4) a step of the type MODE *modename* = *mode*, which defines the new *modename*; the *mode* must include any array size information required when *modename* is used for space generation (at which time it will be evaluated).

module (8) the unit of compilation; in RS systems the three types of module are DECS modules, PROGRAM modules containing an enclosed clause, and PROGRAM modules for composing other PROGRAM modules.

monadic (2.3.2) taking one operand; a monadic operator binds to its operand more tightly than any dyadic operator.

operator (2.3.2) a single or compound symbol or bold word signifying some operation on one or two operands; monadic operators (one operand) bind more tightly than dyadic operators (two operands), which have priorities from 1 (weakest) to 9 (strongest).

operator declaration (5.8) a step of the type OP *operator* = *routine-text*, in which the routine text defines the meaning of the operator for a particular operand mode or pair of modes.

parameter (5.4) an object given as data to a procedure; (formal p~) an identifier used in a routine text to represent such an object; (actual p~) the unit supplied as parameter in a procedure call.

partial composition (8.5.2) a composition module in which one or more holes remain to be filled.

picture (7.5.1) part of a format text capable of describing the external character representation and layout of one value.

primary (*expression*, 2.3.1) a compact item such as an identifier, denotation or enclosed clause, from which larger constructions can be built.

priority (2.3.2) a decimal digit expressing the binding power of a dyadic operator, 1 for the weakest, 9 for the strongest.

priority declaration (5.8) a step of the type PRIO *operator* = *digit*, defining the priority for all dyadic meanings of the operator.

procedure (5) a piece of program defined by a routine text and obeyed by a procedure call; an object whose mode begins PROC; the Algol term for 'subroutine'.

procedure call (*primary*, 5.2) a call for a procedure to be obeyed, i.e. a primary representing the procedure, followed by a list of actual parameters separated by commas and enclosed in parentheses.

program (2.1) an enclosed clause preceded, in RS systems, by PROGRAM *title* and followed by FINISH; (program module, 8) an enclosed clause module or a composition module.

range (3.2) the region of a program over which some particular declaration remains valid, e.g. (in RS systems) the remaining portion of the simple closed clause containing the declaration.

recursion (5.7) the use of a procedure or operator within its own routine text; (mutual r~) the use of two or more procedures which call each other in a circular fashion.

reference (1.3) the linguistic counterpart of a working space in store; a reference is treated as an object in its own right and has a mode beginning REF.

replicator (7.5.3) an integer denotation used in a format text for the purpose of repetition; (dynamic replicator, 7.5.6) a construction of the type n(*series*) to give a computed degree of repetition.

routine text (*unit*, 5.3) the piece of program which defines a procedure or one meaning of an operator.

row (4.2) a one-dimensional array; in a mode, [ ] means 'row of' and [,] is pronounced 'row row of'.

rowing (4.3.2) the coercion which, in strong contexts only, adds 'row' or 'row of' to the mode of an object, e.g. treats an INT as a [ ]INT having just one element.

selection (*expression*, 6.2.1) the construction *selector* OF *primary* or *selector* OF *selection*, which picks out one field from a structure; a selection must be bracketed when parameterized or indexed, but need not be bracketed for use as an operand. [In the formal syntax of Algol 68, a selection is classed as a 'secondary': the rules given here are equivalent.]

selector (6.2.1) part of the mode of a structure having the same form as an identifier and used for selection of one field (see 'selection').

series (2.1) a sequence of steps separated by semi-colons, the final step obeyed (a unit) giving the result of the series.

simple closed clause (*primary*, 3.2) the simplest type of enclosed clause, a series in parentheses or between BEGIN and END.

slice (*primary*, 2.3.1) a construction consisting of a primary representing an array followed by an indexer to pick out one element or some larger subset.

step (2.1) loosely, one simple move in a program; precisely, a declaration or a unit; a component of a series. [The formal Algol 68 term for a step is 'phrase', which seems less descriptive, and is not used in this Guide.]

string (4.4) a row of characters, mode [ ]CHAR, or (more basically in RS systems) a character structure coercible to [ ]CHAR in strong contexts and operand positions.

strong context (1.1) a position in a program in which the required mode of object is completely determined by context, so that all forms of coercion can be applied; typical strong contexts are the right-hand sides of assignments and of identity declarations.

structure (6.2) a composite object having fields of various modes chosen by the programmer; the mode of a structure is of the form STRUCT(*mode selector, mode selector, ...*).

subscript (4.2.2) a unit delivering an integer, used in an indexer to pick out one element from a row (or reduce by one the number of dimensions of a multi-dimensional array).

transput (7) a term covering input and output.

trimmer (4.2.3) a construction used in an indexer to subset one of the dimensions of an array; the form of a trimmer in full is u:v AT w, where u, v and w are units delivering integers.

union (6.8) a mode of the form UNION(*mode, mode,* etc.) to which any objects of a constituent *mode* can be united, enabling objects of various different modes to be treated alike.

unit (2.1) the syntactic class which includes expressions, assignments, routine texts, identity relations and jumps; units are used as right-hand sides of assignments, as parameters in procedure calls, etc., and—interspersed with declarations—as the steps in a program.

uniting (6.8) the coercion applied in strong and operand contexts which replaces an object by a union containing that object.

variable (1.3) an identifier representing a reference; a variable of mode REF INT can hold an INT, and similarly for references to all other modes (including procedures).

variable declaration (2.2.1) a step of the type *mode identifier* or (with initialization) *mode identifier* : = *unit*, which creates working space for an object of the given mode and defines the identifier as the reference to it.

voiding (5.5) the discarding of an object in a strong void context, such as that preceding a semi-colon.

widening (Appendix 2) the coercion in which an object is replaced by a corresponding object having a 'wider' mode e.g. REAL instead of INT, taking place in strong contexts only.

width (7.3.1) the full number of decimal digits required to represent a number such as an integer, the mantissa of a real or the exponent of a real; also the number of characters in a BYTES value or bits in a BITS value.

Index

For operators, see Appendix 3.
Entries not starting with a capital letter are standard identifiers.